TAKING A LEAD

Taking
a
lead

DEREK COPLEY

STL BOOKS
BROMLEY, KENT

KINGSWAY PUBLICATIONS
EASTBOURNE

ISBN 0 86065 360 9
STL ISBN 1 85078 003 X

Unless otherwise indicated, biblical quotations are from the
New International Version, © New York International
Bible Society 1978

Front cover design: Vic Mitchell

STL Books are published by Send the Light
(Operation Mobilisation), P.O. Box 48, Bromley,
Kent, England.

Printed in Great Britain for
KINGSWAY PUBLICATIONS LTD
Lottbridge Drove, Eastbourne, E. Sussex BN23 6NT by
Cox & Wyman Ltd, Reading.
Typeset by CST, Eastbourne.

Contents

Acknowledgement

I am grateful to Mrs Marilyn Hart for her good work in typing the manuscript.

DEREK COPLEY

From One Ordinary Leader to Another . . .

Since I became a Christian in 1958 I have been involved in various kinds of leadership. My first responsibility was leading a small Christian Union group in a student hall of residence. From there I sailed to the United States and did church planting among Whites and American Indians. On my return to the UK in 1966 I led a Bible class for teenagers and later helped to establish a new church in Stockport. In 1970 I was asked to become the Principal of Moorlands Bible College.

Today I exercise leadership at various levels, ranging from the 'top' as Principal of the College, to the pastoral care of a group of eleven students. In my local church I function as an elder.

As I look back over the past twenty-seven years, most of my influence at any one time has been over a relatively small number of people. I have never risen to stardom with its prestige, prominence and superb opportunities to affect thousands of lives. Because of this, I understand what it is like to be an ordinary leader. It is to such men and women that I have written this book. I especially want to encourage those who are inclined to underestimate the value of their own roles. It is with those who say 'I'm only a . . .' that I want to share my heart.

We *are* meant to be influential—but it must be within

the sphere chosen by God, however large or small that may be. You will be encouraged to know that you can expect a 'knock-on' effect. Why? Because that is the way God works, and it is both taught and illustrated in Scripture. Although Jesus did reach out to the multitudes, he focused most of his attention on a small group of twelve. Whether God has appointed you to lead six or six hundred, if you follow the principles of leadership taught in the Bible your sphere of influence will be greater than you think.

Good leadership techniques are important, but our real effectiveness may be more dependent on other things. For example, people will follow those whose lives match their teaching. They will not listen where there is obvious hypocrisy. They will also respond to a leader who is able to communicate God's heart clearly to them.

Only men and women who are close to God will learn his secrets. That is why I have emphasized the need to make our devotional lives top priority. There is little value in being technically competent if we neglect our relationship with God.

Today's leaders need to understand themselves as well as others. We are as human as those we lead. We face enormous pressures created by our own emotional needs, and at the same time we are expected to cater for their needs. The two are in competition. If we fail by putting ourselves first, our effectiveness will be reduced dramatically. We need to know how to cope with such a dilemma.

I used to see leadership as 'getting things done through other people'. That is, a concern primarily with productivity. I now regard its main aim as individual and corporate spiritual growth. The way we handle people will be determined by our understanding of the role of leadership. If we see ourselves as 'bosses' and the people as our 'workforce' we will resort to unbiblical styles of leadership. On the other hand, when we realize that our followers are people who need nurturing, we will be less conscious of our authority and more aware of *their* needs.

A much neglected area of ministry is among our fellow leaders—house-group leaders, elders, deacons and committee members concerned with children, youth and adults. There is always so much urgent business that we fail to build each other up and we become distant in our most vital relationships. I am personally determined to concentrate more effort on ministering among the teams to which I belong.

Those who are led will be less motivated to work for God than those who read this book. We need to know what kind of things hinder their progress, and what we should be doing to inspire them. When we understand the nature of motivation we shall know how to help people to do their best for God.

Most leaders are called by God to bring about change in line with God's will. Even reading the word 'change' may be to some a painful reminder of past disasters. Some will have retreated from the front line, preferring a quiet life. But God has not called us to maintain the status quo but boldly and sensitively to move people on. Christians are like any other people when they are confronted by something new—many feel threatened by it and will put up a fight. We need to remember their humanity and to bear it constantly in mind. This will not guarantee total success, but we are much less likely to run into trouble.

Good organizing and clear planning are essential. But most of all, leadership is about people—their inward feelings and outward reactions, the things they fear and the ventures which excite them. Ours is a great privilege as well as a responsibility. I'm glad I'm a leader and I'm grateful for this special opportunity of sharing my thoughts with you.

DEREK COPLEY

Part 1

THE INFLUENCE OF LEADERSHIP

You are more important than you think.
Whether you have charge of three, ten or
a hundred people, if that is where God
has placed you then work among them.
And expect that the changes in their lives
will in turn affect others.

I

Make Ripples Where You Are

During the three weeks of the 1984 Spring Harvest I conducted seminars on leadership for about 700 people. Although I felt that my teaching was of a good standard, I gradually became aware that I was leaving some of them frustrated. Why? It was because they thought that they didn't have the right position or authority to carry out many of the things I was suggesting. You see, most of them were not pastors but house-group leaders, elders, deacons, youth workers and women's workers. A sense of despair came over me. What hope could I give them that once they arrived home from Prestatyn they would actually be able to influence their churches to any real degree?

One of the things which disturbs me at present is the idea that unless you are a big name, a person with a dynamic personality or somebody who holds a key position in church, you can make no significant impact on other people. We stare in awe and wonder at the star-studded casts on today's platforms and enjoy their sparkling performances. But when we arrive home we feel rather inferior and somewhat deflated. 'What good can I do?' we moan, 'I'm only a house-group leader.'

It's true; big names do have a unique opportunity to change thousands of lives in a single evening. Yet we should not be pessimistic. The most valuable and lasting work for God is being done at grass roots level by ordinary men and women, most of whom will never be famous.

But what is leadership all about? Am I a failure if I don't address vast admiring audiences? Not at all! Our primary task is to help people around us to grow—however few they may be. In-depth influence week by week can only be effective among relatively small numbers. The large-scale gatherings and even the church pulpit are invaluable for teaching, inspiring and challenging people, but God needs us lesser mortals to look after people day by day.

How do we do that? By being servants to those entrusted to our care. There is a great deal of *talk* about servanthood today. Unfortunately the real emphasis is often on seeking authority and personal power. We refer to 'upside-down pyramids', where we claim that the leaders serve from underneath; whereas in practice it is sometimes the other way round. So what matters most? Being a somebody, a high-powered change agent, having recognized authority. . . or getting on with the job God has given us, content to stay within the sphere of his choice? We should be grateful for those specially anointed national leaders, but let us not feel that we have to try to step into their shoes.

'But don't you have to have *some* special authority to get a hearing?', you might ask. Well, yes and no. It's true that if you are a pastor or a full-time elder you do have unique opportunities to reach more people. But real authority doesn't rely on power or position. It comes from what we are as persons. It's not whom we say we are or feel we are, but whether people see our Christ-likeness. Whether we chat with two people in a living room or address a hundred, what really matters is that we speak 'the very words of God' (1 Pet 4:11). If not, then our real influence will be very limited, however high up we may be. Eventually those who seek power for its own sake without God-given authority will be found out.

We could think of a church as a pond, and its many leaders as stones being tossed into it. Some stones are larger and make bigger ripples. Others are smaller and their gentle ripples don't spread quite so far. So what size stone are you? A full time pastor, perhaps. Your ripples will spread across the whole pond—an awesome responsibility. Perhaps a Sunday School teacher? Then serve your children by your life, teaching and pastoral visitation. Children are as important as adults and need to grow spiritually. Where else do your ripples go? They touch your fellow teachers. Are you a house-group leader? In that case you have the opportunity to exercise considerable spiritual influence among ten or fifteen people.

If God wants us to have more so-called 'power' then he will push us into it. We have no need to seek it. If we live close to God, then we will carry the greatest authority of all—that of being an example which others will follow. If we make ripples where we are, by focusing on the nurture of those nearest to us in the pond, we will not only see them change but also others who are outside our own immediate sphere of influence.

Chain reactions

Much of the electricity in the Western world comes from nuclear power stations. They are similar to oil or coal fired plants except that the heat comes from an atomic reaction rather than burning the fossil fuel. The core of a reactor gets hot because a chain reaction is taking place inside the nuclear fuel rods. As one small particle of matter is released from an atom, it strikes a neighbouring atom and it in turn loses part of itself which collides with another atom, and so on. Each time this happens heat is given out and eventually that heat is converted into electricity.

In a church community one of the ways in which it grows towards maturity is by a series of spiritual chain reactions. As one person's life influences someone else, so he changes inwardly; and he in turn becomes a person whose life affects others—just like an atomic power plant. The most effective leaders are those who start chain reactions by being people whose lives are so godly that those who rub shoulders with them become like them. In theory at least (and often in practice) it needs only one person in a church to cause changes in the lives of many more.

One of the most remarkable examples of this is in the New Testament Thessalonian church. A series of events was sparked off by just three missionaries—Paul, Silas and Timothy—who had been deeply involved for some time in the life of the church. As the people got to know them and observed their lives, they began to resemble the missionaries—'You became imitators of us,' says Paul in 1 Thessalonians 1:6. They admired Paul, Silas and Timothy so much that their own lifestyles and attitudes became very similar. Their influence was not just among one or two, but throughout most of the church—proving that it *is* possible for a small number to be responsible for changes in many more.

It didn't end there. The church gained a good reputation all over Macedonia and Achaia to such a degree that the Thessalonian church became a prototype for others to follow. 'And so you became a model to all the believers in Macedonia and Achaia' (1 Thess 1:7). Even more followed! Paul says: 'Your faith in God has become known everywhere' (1 Thess 1:8). What a chain reaction!

However, it would be unwise to base everything on just one example from the early church. So let's look first at the example of Jesus Christ, and then examine some extended New Testament teaching. In each case we find a chain reaction.

The Lord Jesus was sent by his Father into the world. He in turn sent his disciples, and gave them the Great Commission which was an instruction to all Christians to go into the world to make disciples (Jn 17:18; Mt 28:19-20). Similarly the first link in the chain reaction of love was that Jesus was loved by his Father. He then loved the disciples (Jn 15:9). Finally he ensured that the chain would continue by urging his disciples to love each other (Jn 15:12).

An ever-increasing tidal wave of love was encouraged by Paul in the Thessalonian church: 'May the Lord make your love increase and overflow for each other and for everyone else, just as ours does for you' (1 Thess 3:12). The basis of his exhortation was that Paul, Silas and Timothy had created the first link in the chain reaction by showing deep love towards them. Now he wanted them to follow their example by loving each other.

Paul the apostle taught that Christian lifestyle should be propagated through a chain reaction. 'Follow my example, as I follow the example of Christ' (1 Cor 11:1). Because he could claim with a clear conscience to be a follower of Christ (and had become Christ-like), he could tell others to be like himself by using him as a model to observe and duplicate.

Paul also believed in the chain-reaction concept in the realm of teaching. He first received his teaching from Christ. It was then passed on to Timothy, and he in turn was to teach what he had heard to other instructors who would then themselves pass it on (2 Tim 2:2).

The only way to get a chain reaction going is to be a true example of what we want other people to be, however few may be observing us at present. They will change inwardly; and in turn they will be noticed by others.

How to act as a model

Why is modelling so effective?

First and foremost it works because it is one of God's ways of bringing about growth and change in people's lives. And whenever you obey the instructions of the Bible you can guarantee the results.

Second, all human beings are, at heart, imitators. I'm not referring merely to mimicry or play acting (which are external) but to actual inward change as a result of close long-term exposure to other people's lives, and to society's trends and ideas (communicated through conversations, TV, radio and the printed page).

All children imitate their parents. It's often quite a shock to see the little horrors using our everyday expression and even our worst mannerisms. We don't need to teach them these things—they simply pick them up without either of us being aware of it. When our children were younger my wife used to tell me 'It's bad enough having you around without having a little daddy as well!' She was referring to our son David.

People in peer groups like to be the same as the rest of the crowd. My teenage daughter Sarah and her friend Karen often dress exactly alike and even think alike, because they spend a great deal of time together. My generation hasn't a clue about which pop group is where in the charts, but my son David keeps up with his friends by knowing all the details. And they all seem to wear the same kind of boots—'Doc Martins'.

Imitation is both inward and outward. Inward influences are not always obvious but are nevertheless powerful. In particular we have all absorbed many of our parents' attitudes. Some of them in later life, we would like to get rid of but can't, though we gratefully retain other more useful and helpful parental attitudes.

I have inherited two qualities from my father—one

good and the other something of a nuisance at times. At a very early age I developed a love of gardening, because I observed his intense interest in growing vegetables and flowers. I used to watch him for hours and helped him when I was old enough. Much of what he taught me I now put to use in my own garden.

The other habit I developed was a good sense of reliability and time-keeping. Even now I am rarely late for anything, and I do not let people down if it can be avoided. But it has its drawbacks too. I get angry and uptight when other people aren't as punctual or reliable as I am; and this affects my attitude to them as persons, and can spoil relationships. Freeing myself from this bondage, of everything having to be done properly and on time, is an uphill task.

The same situations happen in a church as relationships develop. We influence each other, for good or bad. If it's for good, then we build each other up. If it's for bad we drag one another down. Paul illustrates this by comparing the bad influences in Ephesus to gangrene. Chain reactions can be powerfully destructive, as well as being a dynamic force for change and growth.

As leaders we hope that people will respond to us. There are two things which will encourage them to do so. First, we must be the kind of people from whom they will truly receive benefit if they follow our example. Second, our teaching and Christian character must match up. If they don't, those whom we lead will come to the conclusion that we are hypocrites, and we will have to resort to some other means to motivate them such as bullying or emotional blackmail.

Being the kind of person they will want to listen to

Let me give you some examples of the power of model lives. Paul's new life was so dramatically different from his old one, that unbelievers who saw it obeyed the gospel

—on the grounds that since God could rescue even Paul, then they themselves were not beyond God's grace (1 Tim 1:16). Many of those who saw the transformed Paul actually turned to Christ.

According to Hebrews 6:12 some of the Christians were in danger of becoming lazy and the writer wanted to encourage them to work harder. How did he persuade them? By lambasting them and laying down the law? No, by telling them to observe those in the church who were models of faith and patience, and to imitate them.

In New Testament days the believers in Judea had suffered terribly for their faith. The remarkable way they endured it, and at the same time grew spiritually, made a big impact on the Thessalonian church. As a result of what they had learned they based their own attitude to suffering on that of the Judeans (1 Thess 2:14).

I don't believe it is irreverent to say that the Lord Jesus was an imitator of a model life—that of his heavenly Father. He observed what his Father was doing and then proceeded to do the same. 'The Son can do nothing by himself; he can only do what he sees his Father doing, because whatever the Father does the Son also does. For the Father loves the Son and shows him all he does' (Jn 5:19-20).

Jesus' life was an excellent example to the disciples. As they worked alongside him day after day, they recognized that he was someone worth listening to and chose to obey him regardless of the cost.

Although Paul admitted that he was the worst of sinners, he also knew that he could with a clear conscience encourage others to become like him and to expect their obedience. He had the kind of personal qualities which would benefit others if they imitated him. 'Therefore I urge you to imitate me. For this reason I am sending to you Timothy' (1 Cor 4:16; see also 1 Cor 11:1).

The elders' and deacons' qualifications in 1 Timothy 3

contain more than the leadership skills necessary for them to do their jobs. The lists are also concerned with character. This again confirms that we need much more than an official title or correct qualifications to be effective leaders. We especially need to be the kind of people whom others will respect and will therefore voluntarily respond to what we say.

Agreement of teaching and character

Hearing and seeing have always been a powerful combination for persuading people. God's Spirit used this in the early church as a tool for evangelism. As Acts 8:6 says: 'When the crowds heard Philip and saw the miraculous signs he did, they all paid close attention to what he said.' Throughout that era the preaching of the gospel was backed up by miracles and as a result many people came to Christ.

Many of you reading this book will not have the opportunity to teach from the pulpit. Yet you still have the privilege and responsibility of guiding others towards understanding and applying the Bible to their daily lives. It is not enough to focus only on the meaning of the Bible, even though it is the only basis for good Christian living. We must also help people to live their lives in accordance with that doctrine (Tit 2:1). If they are to apply biblical teaching to the practical issues of life, we must find the right way to encourage them to respond to our instruction.

People will listen when our lives and teaching are consistent with each other and when they can discern clearly that God is actually speaking through us. In their dispute with Paul the rebellious Corinthians failed to respond to Paul because, they claimed, Paul had not given adequate proof that Christ was speaking through him. It is obvious that Paul had been a channel for God's voice. Probably they had no intention of listening anyway. But an important point had been made; that when a leader does speak with God's voice, he or she ought reasonably to expect people to take notice (1 Cor 13:2-4).

Peter puts this very plainly. 'If anyone speaks, he should do it as one speaking the very words of God' (1 Pet 4:11). It is true that even when people do hear God speaking through us they can still choose to ignore us— but they are much less likely to do so.

Where the real power lies

The real power to lead depends on the depth and reality with which the Word we teach is seen to be alive in our daily Christian lives. Technically it's called the Incarnational Principle. It is rather like Paul's reference to the Corinthian believers as living letters. When people saw their lives they 'read' a message from Paul. The way they lived spoke as clearly as if Paul had actually written them a real letter. No ink or tablets of stone were needed to communicate effectively; just transformed lives (2 Cor 3:1-3).

One of the plainest and boldest statements about this was made by Paul: 'I urge you to imitate me. For this reason I am sending to you Timothy . . . . He will remind you of my way of life in Christ Jesus, which agrees with what I teach everywhere in every church' (1 Cor 4:16-17). Similarly in Hebrews 13:17 the writer urged his hearers to imitate the faith of their leaders, on the basis of the relationship between their spoken word and way of life. 'Remember your leaders who spoke the word of God to you. Consider the outcome of their way of life and imitate their faith.'

When we actually model the truths we teach, we can expect people to follow our instruction, because the word of God is powerful. Paul, in trying to encourage a rather timid Timothy to continue his ministry, told him to command and teach but to reinforce it by setting an example. Then he could expect that people would listen (1 Tim

4:11-12). Indeed Paul used this principle with Timothy
—he not only gave him good advice (which was worth
following in itself) but he also told Timothy to consider
the reputation of the one writing to him. 'You, however,
know all about my teaching, my way of life . . . . But as
for you, continue in what you have learned . . . because
you know those from whom you learned it' (2 Tim 3:10,
14).

In his exhortation to the Thessalonians Paul appealed
to them to obey because he knew that they had clearly
observed his life and in their heart of hearts knew he was a
person who was approved by God. Therefore, they would
be quite safe in heeding his message (1 Thess 2:3–6).

Leadership—character as much as gift or position

The New Testament emphasizes leadership skills and
competence. But it stresses even more the character of
the person who leads. Paul was certainly a good teacher
and was able to communicate clearly and effectively. Yet
he urged people to respond to what they had *seen* in him
as well as learned and heard from him in his capacity as a
teacher (Phil 4:9).

Rank does have its importance. Sometimes it may be
appropriate to remind people of our God-appointed
position in the church, in order to motivate them to respond to us. Paul did this in most of his epistles. A notable
exception is the letter to the church in Thessalonica, where
he probably had his closest relationships. Here he did
not quote his official authority as a basis for persuading
them to obey. Rather, he appealed to their knowledge of
his personal integrity. The kind of person he was, was far
more impressive than his apostleship.

Despite his position as a pastor in Ephesus, Timothy
was in real danger of being ignored because of his timidity
and relative youth (he was probably in his mid-thirties).
Paul's advice was that he should thoroughly reinforce

what he taught by setting 'an example for the believers in speech, in life, in love, in faith and in purity' (1 Tim 4:12). In other words, his real authority lay in the fact that he was personally demonstrating the truths he was teaching, rather than in the significance of the office that he held.

How do you become a model Christian?

'All this theory and doctrine is fine,' you might say, 'but what can I *do* to become the kind of person others will follow?'

I believe that the fastest personal transformation occurs when there is a balance between our effort and God working in us. (This is illustrated by Paul's statement in 1 Corinthians 15:10, 'I worked harder than all of them— yet not I, but the grace of God that was with me.') We will probably be disappointed if we simply wait around for God to do it all. We must make personal efforts to develop those character traits which will influence people.

I do a great deal of reading in the areas of ministry in which I am involved. I have learnt a lot from what others have written as a result of their personal experiences in leadership. I don't mean just learning about the 'nuts and bolts', like delegation and job descriptions, but also about qualities like loyalty, openness, optimism, trust- worthiness and self-discipline. Dare I mention 'self- improvement' courses which are sometimes run in the UK for Christians? 'Yuk,' you say, 'it sounds like an encouragement to human effort, denying the power of God.' Yes, I agree it does, but it's not meant to. I'm just reminding you that a coin has two sides, the other one being the power of God without which we will never change.

Reading has helped me in other areas too, such as how to respond more maturely to criticism and compliments. There have been many occasions when I have handled both these badly. Reading will help us to amend many aspects of our character and work so that we will have a better credit rating among those we serve. I'm not thinking of anything deceptive like trying to project an 'image', but of becoming the man or woman who will command respect by virtue of his or her character. In Britain we are beginning to see the emergence of conferences especially designed for leaders, such as Leadership '84. There is a tremendous advantage in being taught the skills and spiritual dimensions of leadership by those who are already effective leaders.

I would strongly recommend the investment of time and money in courses and conferences. Perhaps your church would consider sponsoring you to attend such an event. Our own pastor and his wife go to at least one conference a year at the church's expense.

Mixing with models

I hope that I have established the principle that people will change for the better (or worse) when they model their lives on those of leaders such as yourself. That same process ought to occur in our own lives too—the more we are in close contact with the right kind of people the more *we* will change and then become good examples for others.

The Thessalonians based their lives on two kinds of model—other people, and God himself. 'You became imitators of us [Paul, Silas and Timothy] and of the Lord' (1 Thess 1:6). He told the Corinthians to do the same— 'Follow my example, as I follow the example of Christ' (1 Cor 11:1). And Paul instructed the Ephesians to 'Be imitators of God' (Eph 5:1).

Let us consider the chain reaction:-
                    God the Father. . .
                    God the Son. . .
                    Other models whom we follow. . .

Ourselves. . .

Those who follow us.

Jesus learnt from his Father by observation and fellowship. He did what he saw his Father doing. He nurtured that special relationship continually. To be that next vital link we must do the same. Jesus appointed the twelve to preach and to have authority to drive out demons (Mk 3:14), but the same verse tells us of a more important activity—'that they might be with him'. To become like Christ takes time and effort. Even after three years of intensive fellowship the disciples were far from perfect. No one can imitate God by mimicry or play-acting—it has to be inward and gradual, and is usually costly.

To mould our lives blindly and exclusively on just one or two humans would be dangerous. That's why Paul commended the Thessalonians for basing their lives on God as well as himself. We must do the same. We must remember that people make mistakes and that it is unwise to put them on pedestals.

Yet the idea of spending time with those who are positive and of like mind is utterly biblical. Paul wrote about 'joining with others' in Philippians 3:17 and 'fleeing *along* with those' (2 Tim 2:22, my italics). The more we mix with such people the more they will influence our lives.

In the past twenty-six years of my Christian life I can recall with gratitude a handful of men and women who have made a real impact on my life. Soon after my conversion in 1958 I met John and Grace Wyatt in Stockport —godly, stable, dependable, patient and generous people. A few years later I met an American evangelist, Worth Ellis, a man who fired me with zeal for preaching Christ among American Indians. More recently there has been Doug Barnett whose optimism and positive thinking has been a challenge to my rather pessimistic outlook. I want to mention my good friend Clive Calver with his almost inexhaustible supplies of energy and drive

—a man who gets things done. Finally, I am grateful for meeting Reg and Lucia East (fomerly of the Barnabas Fellowship, Whatcombe House). My own counselling still reflects what I learnt from them as I observed their gentle but firm approach.

Me in my small corner

I would like to suggest that you forget the limitations imposed by your sphere of service and focus constructively on your section of the pond. You are probably more important than you think. People like yourself are the backbone of today's churches. Perhaps you will not turn the world upside down; but you can be vitally involved at local level—causing growth in others on an increasing scale. And, who knows, your church may become a prototype in your district, your county, or even further afield.

Part 2

THE PREPARATION FOR LEADERSHIP

People expect you to know what is on God's heart and to help them to know what he is thinking. Your personal relationship with God is the basis for being able to hear God's voice more clearly.

They will look to you to meet their many unmet needs and to sacrifice yours. You should be aware of which of your own needs are fighting to be fulfilled.

2

A Leader's Devotional Life

My 18,000-mile pastoral and teaching tour of Asia had taken eighteen months to plan. Considering the uncertainties of third-world travel, things had gone quite well in India and Nepal. So I confidently expected that in Pakistan I would travel by air—hopping from one location to another across the Sind desert from Karachi right up to Lahore in the Punjab. But that was not to be. Only one flight had actually been booked, from Multan to Lahore. Unfortunately its arrival time had clashed with the departure of my flight from Lahore to Delhi, so it was cancelled. After much confusion it was decided that I should go by bus and train instead.

The air-conditioned coach from Karachi to Hyderabad was excellent and so was the road surface. But the journey from Hyderabad to a small desert town called Kunri was something of a nightmare. A Landrover had been sent all the way from Kunri to pick me up, but had broken down and was beyond repair. There was no choice but to go by ordinary Pakistani service bus. No air-conditioning this time, and for much of the journey not much solid road either.

It was incredibly hot. Though it had cooled down considerably, it was still 108 °F. in the shade, and the bus became a stifling oven as we lurched across the bumps at an average of fifteen miles per hour. It was not only scorching, but dry and dusty too. Some places had seen no rain for five years, so there was little vegetation. Out there in the burning sand lay the bleached bones of animals that had been picked clean by the vultures which constantly wheeled around overhead.

Day turned into night. It was scary because that part of Pakistan is well known for its snakes and its bandits. Once we broke down but got going again. Another time we came up against a totally blocked track where two vehicles had collided. Eventually we rolled into Kunri. Even though it was dark I could see that the desert had suddenly disappeared and had given way to lush vegetation. Next morning revealed the glorious sight of tall trees, bushes with brightly coloured flowers and luscious tropical fruits.

Why was it so green? The answer is that it was irrigated by one of the enormous canals, which criss-cross the desert. Everywhere I went there was the same sharp contrast, between the dry and dusty land and the vegetation that flourished wherever there was water.

I have often thought about those vivid scenes. They remind me of the vast differences between the devotional lives of my Christian friends involved in leadership.

Some are flourishing. For them the Bible is alive and relevant. They read it eagerly each day. Their prayer times are a joy because their relationship with God is warm and rich. They look forward to conversations with their heavenly Father; God is so real and accessible. Their spiritual appetite is enormous and they take in all that God provides.

But there are others whose spiritual lives are just like a desert. Often their quiet times are motivated only by a sense of guilt, and they go through the motions with reluctance and apathy. Some are energetically working at it, yet despite their enormous efforts, their hoped-for richness never comes. Sadly, there are far too many who have given up altogether.

What is so tragic is that spiritual dryness prevents us from refreshing others and building them up. Some of us who are leaders are not delivering the goods as far as the 'led' are concerned. To impoverish our own Christian lives is bad enough, but to deprive others too is spiritually criminal. Hundreds of thousands of believers are looking to us, and from some of us they deserve a better deal.

Like those evil grey vultures in Asia who search for flesh, our 'enemy the devil prowls around like a roaring lion looking for someone to devour' (1 Pet 5:8). Weary and spiritually listless leaders are easy prey for Satan. And once your devotional life has all but dried up you're well on the way to becoming a powerless Christian. You can still be very active in church or in evangelism, but you're no longer an effective channel of blessing to others. Even worse, you could end up as a nominal churchgoer, or even a backslider.

Dryness creates a vicious circle. If our quiet times are poor, the other hours of the day will be affected too. And that general lack of spiritual vitality takes away our appetite for Bible meditation and prayer. So our Christian lives spiral downwards, each month being worse than the last.

How can leaders end up so dry?

Some Christians have always felt an uncomfortable lack of spiritual depth in their lives. Despite their best efforts they have never really experienced much of the reality of the presence, power and love of God. Others used to enjoy real closeness and warmth in their relationship with him, but for various reasons it has ebbed away.

While we mustn't use them as excuses, there are some valid reasons why quiet times sometimes decline in quality or quantity.

A good number of us are not getting enough spiritual nourishment. Those who work shifts or unsocial hours find it hard to get to church regularly. The same might be true of those who teach Sunday School while the sermon is being preached, or who have to baby-sit while their partner goes to church. Those who preach and teach often spend most of their time giving out rather than taking in.

Sometimes it is impossible to organize a fixed time each day to pray (like parents with young children or travelling evangelists). On the other hand our own lack of self-discipline may be the cause. Unemployed people, who ought to have lots of free time, often find that their unstructured day affects their attempts to establish the habit of a daily quiet time.

There are times when particular pressures or personal problems seem to preoccupy us and take away our interest in prayer. This happens despite the fact that we know we should spend even more time with God.

So many active Christians today are just tired out. It is certainly true of those who are involved in 'full time service'—have you ever seen the diary of an itinerant evangelist or a pastor? But it is equally applicable to people with jobs, or with families to look after—their service for God has to be fitted in on top of their careers and family responsibilities. Often those who are successful in their jobs, or take responsibilities to their neighbours seriously, are called upon to do more than most in their churches.

For those who preach, teach or lead, where hours of preparation are needed, there is a big temptation to use the devotional time as a study period instead. I can remember struggling with this issue at Royal Week when I was doing seminars on the Book of Romans. I had set aside 6.30-8.30 a.m. for my quiet time and final preparation for my lectures. Each morning I had to force myself to have a proper time of prayer instead of using the whole two hours for a last look through my notes.

I have discovered that setbacks and failures in people's jobs or Christian work can cause them to have a chip on their shoulder. Sometimes they develop a wrong perspective on God. When we're in that frame of mind we think of God as mean, uncaring and unjust because he has allowed things to go badly in spite of our consecration.

Surprisingly, success in our career, home life or Christian service can also lead to our becoming slack about our quiet time. It's so easy to ride on the crest of a wave, when everything we touch seems to turn to gold, and prayer seems hardly necessary. Our joy and elation seem to be sufficient to carry us along. The danger is that when things become less exciting or even unpleasant, there is no firm foundation to help us cope with the darker days.

Are quiet times necessary anyway?

The fact that so many of us neglect them or ignore them altogether does seem to indicate that we don't regard them as terribly important. Is our attitude correct? Have we at last found a way of holiness and growth that has outdated the rather old-fashioned approach?

Today some Christians are saying that you really don't need a specific time set aside for prayer and Bible study, because you can know the presence of God all day. They say we can take in the Bible by listening to sermons, reading books or hearing taped ministry.

In one sense these things are true. And I would have to agree that the Bible does not say how or when we are to pray or read the Scriptures. Yet when I hear people say something like 'I've been liberated from my quiet time since I now possess the Spirit's fullness', I shudder.

I shudder because 99% of the Christians I know would

probably backslide if they followed such ideas. Perhaps a very special few can survive without a time set aside each day, but if so, it is only a few. Of course I don't doubt the need to cultivate the presence of God at all times of the day. Yet I don't believe it can replace the discipline of spending time just talking to God. A great many aspects of the prayer lives of the men and women of the Bible would probably not have developed casually while they were going about everyday business. It is clear too that they must have studied in depth and meditated on the Scriptures.

If our devotional times are regularly legalistic, boring and dry, then something is wrong, but to abandon them altogether, or to get them over with in ten minutes, is not the answer. Many aspects of growth and achievement in our Christian lives will not occur automatically without the pain and effort of wrestling in prayer or being deeply challenged by the Bible. If these things are to happen, we need to concentrate solely on the task in hand. They won't happen very often while we're driving the car or doing the shopping.

What is the purpose of a quiet time?

A devotional time has many facets and phases. No two days will ever be identical, nor will the experience of two different people. There will be times of praise and worship. Sometimes we will be seeking God's help with a problem about relationships. Sometimes there will be weaknesses in our lives and we will need God's help, or we might seek his guidance about our jobs or some other decision.

But first and foremost, spending time with God is all about a relationship. A missionary in Pakistan wrote in her prayer letter after several years of service, 'I've just discovered that God cares more about my relationship with him than my service for him.' What a discovery! At a meeting of evangelists in 1983, David Watson described on tape how he assessed his life's priorities following the discovery that he had incurable cancer. He realized that his full diary had to some extent hindered his progress in knowing God. During the months that followed, his illness forced him to cut down on his Christian activities, and he was then able to use the time freed to concentrate on his relationship with God.

Some of us need to make major changes in our schedules and lifestyles. It can often be painful and difficult. We're only likely to do it once we're convinced that a higher proportion of time and energy should be devoted to knowing God.

There is no competition between the devotional life and active service. Both are important. It is all a question of priorities. Whatever else we may do, our relationship with God must come first. After that, what we do for God will be enriched, because it will be done as a result of that growing relationship. The more we enjoy God, the more gladly we'll work for him.

Two incidents in the life of Mary illustrate this—sitting at Jesus' feet in Luke 10:38-44, and anointing him with ointment in John 12:1-8. On both occasions she was criticized because others believed that service was more important. Martha thought she should have been serving instead, and Judas said that the ointment should have been turned into money for the poor.

Jesus himself said, 'It is enough for the student to be like his teacher, and the servant like his master' (Mt 10:24). We do exist to serve him, because we have committed ourselves to doing his will when we become his disciples. But we are especially to become like him. Have you noticed that couples who have been married a long time sometimes look alike? It usually only happens when there has been a close and happy relationship. Characteristics of one rub off on the other. If we are to become like Christ, we must spend time together. The richness of that time as well as the length of it is important. The appreciation of God's love may occur at any time of the day or in a church service, but so often it is when we're quietly alone with him that the Spirit opens our hearts and floods us with his love (Rom 5:5).

A leader's job is to influence others so that they will grow. We can only do this effectively if they consider that we are worth listening to. A man or woman who is moving towards Christ-likeness can expect others to accept his or her teaching and help, because it is backed up by a life which is an example of what we want them to become.

3

Building a Richer Devotional Life

During my time in Asia, I met over 200 missionaries. I wasn't able to talk to all of them in depth because I often had no more than twenty-four hours in one place. Of all those who did seek my help and advice, a fair proportion had serious devotional problems. Dryness, with a subsequent lack of motivation, was the most common complaint. That surprised me because I had assumed that this was the one area which missionaries would have got sorted out long ago.

But what they were looking for was a formula, a Bible verse or a pat answer to solve their problems. I could produce no such painless remedy. I advised some to change their lifestyle; others simply needed more self-discipline. A few had never fully known the rich experience of the love of God, and we prayed for the Spirit to unlock the pathways to that love.

Yes, even missionaries struggle. And so do evangelists, pastors, youth workers, house-group leaders and Sunday School teachers. (And Bible College principals!) Both the leaders and the led find this to be the greatest area of challenge. If only it were not accompanied by a sense of failure and guilt! Wouldn't it be nice if someone did discover an instant solution?

In late 1983 I talked to 280 evangelists about their

devotional lives. I felt something of a hypocrite and a fraud, because plenary speakers are supposed to be experts in the subject they expound. I offered no easy cure then, nor can I do so now. But I do have some suggestions which might help us to take the right steps to improve or rebuild our quiet time.

Improving our quiet times

'A change is as good as a rest' is a common expression. It applies to everyday life in all sorts of ways. Even good habits become dull routine eventually. A new way of doing things is often all we need. Devotionally, it's quite a good idea to change things round a bit every three to six months. We could switch from one set of daily Bible reading notes to another, or even use none at all for a while in order to go through the Bible without following someone else's plan. Perhaps you are one of those Christians who have never read the Bible through in its entirety. If that is so, perhaps in addition to your deeper meditation on just a few verses, you could find another part of the day to read several chapters, and so cover the entire Bible at least once every year or two.

Our prayer lives might benefit from either more structure or less. Those who find their praying has become rather aimless might adopt various suggestions from books on prayer, or seek advice from those who do not have that problem. On the other hand, Christians who have become rigid and restricted by too much structure may need to experiment with freer forms of prayer.

Where our devotional lives have been given an inadequate amount of time and indiscipline is not the culprit, measures must be taken to give the Bible and prayer a higher priority. We are often encouraged to rearrange things in order to give more time to our friends, parents and families, so why not in this vital area of relationship?

Sometimes the changes have to be quite drastic to be effective and are often misunderstood by others. But whatever else we make time for, we must create opportunities to talk to God and to slow down long enough to listen to him, whatever the cost.

For someone whose quiet time has virtually vanished or is reduced to a quick prayer on the way to the station, it may be embarrassing to explain why he or she is suddenly getting up earlier in the morning. Equally, to plan on being less busy and overcommitted in church will not always be welcome; some jobs won't get done, or a greater load will be borne by others.

Why do we take on so much? Maybe people put pressure on us by manipulating us through emotional or spiritual blackmail. Some of us simply can't say no, either because we're afraid of people's reactions or because we're responding to the need to be needed. For those in full-time Christian service who work 'independently' or are paid an inadequate salary, there is strong financial pressure to keep a full diary in order to survive.

Some of my friends benefit enormously from occasionally taking a whole day off just to be alone with God. It needs to be planned carefully, otherwise we may begin by praying for fifteen minutes and then wonder what to do next! It may be possible to use several days, or even weeks, for a mini retreat or sabbatical. There is an increasing number of communities and quiet centres which cater especially for the busy Christian who needs time to recuperate spiritually, emotionally and physically.

When I wrote in the previous chapter that communion with God as we go about everyday life cannot replace a quiet time, I was not belittling that level of fellowship. Some of us would do well to cultivate the habit of quietly enjoying God's presence all day long. This is especially true for those who feel that God can only be available between 6.30 and 7.15 a.m. when they 'officially' talk to him.

God is there all the time, but being able to appreciate his continual presence isn't something that comes to us overnight. Although I'm still struggling to learn how to do it, I'm slowly winning. If what I'm doing doesn't require too much concentration I sometimes play a tape of Scripture songs. Recently I was sharply reminded that I could profitably use any spare moments to commune with God. A student arrived ten minutes late for an appointment and I was a little irritated. Her reply challenged me: 'Well, you could have spent the time praying instead of sitting there fuming.'

Rebuilding the ruins

Some devotional lives need more than a few improvements. They need rebuilding from scratch. In 1977 after nineteen years as a Christian, having successfully led the re-establishment of a major Bible College and having been involved in planting six churches, I was near spiritual bankruptcy. In some people's eyes I had become a 'somebody', but as far as God was concerned I had little interest in knowing him more deeply. For years, my energy, spurred on by spectacular growth at Moorlands, kept me going. But to me, God was still rather cold and unreal. He was somewhere 'out there' to be served rather than known intimately.

The spiritual lives and warmth of many students put me to shame as I struggled to maintain my two minute quiet time. Only with the gentle transforming help of the Holy Spirit did I respond to the challenge of those beautiful young lives. I find it somewhat humiliating to have to admit all this, but I'm so glad I began to rebuild the ruins, because it has changed my life, my relationship with God and people, and my ministry.

I realize now that Jesus is ready to meet the needs of Christians who thirst after a deeper life, as well as providing for unbelievers who are seeking salvation. The power of the Spirit is available to change the dry and meaningless life into one of warmth and richness, just as he did mine, but . . . .

God usually asks for an effort on our part. Whether it's problem solving, seeking guidance, strengthening a gift or transforming a quiet time, those who are the most determined and persistent will experience the fastest and deepest work of God. It may mean having a quiet time even before we feel motivated, and even when it doesn't make sense at first.

We need each other too

Sometimes the improving or rebuilding involves working it through alone with God, asking that as we take the right steps he will provide the necessary motivation and results to spur us on.

Often God wants us to accept help from people too. I suppose this must be the one area of our Christian lives where we'd prefer not to seek help, because it's too personal, and too embarrassing even to admit that there's a problem. When we need practical help like moving chairs or providing a buffet tea, we have no difficulty asking people to help. Nor would we feel too bad about seeking an explanation of a difficult doctrine or being taught how to give a children's talk.

But I have discovered that quiet times are a taboo subject! In my preparation for that evangelist's conference I wrote to fifteen friends about their devotional lives. Some skipped the issue altogether. Others felt free to be more honest. When I asked what they considered to be the areas of weakness among other evangelists, I got replies such as 'I don't recall a conversation along those lines . . . but that's the biggest point of all . . . none of us likes to admit his or her weaknesses to each other!'

Even among that close fraternity of evangelists there appeared to be very little sharing in this vital area. I suspect that many of us would love to discuss it if only we could pluck up the courage to raise the subject. Sadly, we keep it bottled up inside us like a guilty secret—no one must ever know. So we fail to get help from our closest friends; and we rob them of the opportunity to minister to us, because we're very uncomfortable being served.

It takes real humility and courage to seek someone's advice and to ask him or her to pray with us. It's risky too, because we may get a negative reaction or a few trite Bible verses thrown at us. If you are in need, may I suggest that you visit, write or telephone someone you trust, and whom you know is currently enjoying a rich relationship with God?

Conversely, if you are fortunate enough to be having good quiet times, you might ask God to help you to be alert to anyone in your church who is experiencing a spiritual dryness, and then make a tactful approach. Most people hide their true feelings, but with God's power we ought to be able to discern those in distress.

*　　*　　*

There are so many benefits of a successful devotional life that it's quite impossible to write about all of them. However there are two aspects which are well worth considering. The first concerns the stability of our Christian lives. It is essential that it should be based on something much more solid than the daily ups and downs we experience. The second is about serving God. We are to serve God as well as know and love him. They are not in competition. The devotional life has a vital contribution to make in releasing the resources we need to work for God.

Keeping our lives steady

Life's 'downs' caused by pressure, personal problems, discouragement, failure or hardships can affect us so severely that we begin to get a wrong view of God and Christian service. The writer of Psalm 73 recalls the time when he had a grieved heart and an embittered spirit against God and holiness (vv. 13,21). As a result of allowing his outlook on life to be controlled by his hardships and struggles he became spiritually 'senseless and ignorant' (v. 22). He had become like a brute beast before God (v. 22).

In times of stress our understanding can become cloudy and distorted and we, feel as confused as the psalmist— 'When I tried to understand all this, it was oppressive to me' (v. 16). We begin to ask ourselves whether all this prayer, Bible study, hard work and obedience is really worthwhile when so many things seem to go wrong. We even begin to think unworthy thoughts like 'Surely in vain have I kept my heart pure' (v. 13). It's even worse when we see other people neglecting their Christian lives and apparently getting away with it. We may find an echo in our own hearts of v. 12—'This is what the wicked are like— always carefree, they increase in wealth.' Before long we begin to drift away from God—'But as for me, my feet had almost slipped; I had nearly lost my foothold' (v. 2).

Fortunately the psalmist realized just in time how to get his perspectives right again, and he 'entered the sanctuary of God' (v. 17). Only then did it all begin to make sense. He concludes the psalm by acknowledging, 'But as for me, it is good to be near God. I have made the Sovereign Lord my refuge' (v. 28).

Almost the worst thing possible happened to David— his best friends were talking of stoning him. What did he do? Did he become bitter against God? No, he 'found strength in the Lord his God' (1 Sam 30:6). Despite his total bewilderment, David clung to the very person whom deep down he knew really did care, even though he had apparently abandoned him.

When things are at their worst and we are the least inclined to spend time with God, it's especially then that we need to do just that. In a sense we have no alternative but to walk with faith until the picture clears. Paul must have done this during his terrible ordeals in Philippi. Later, as he looked back on those awful incidents he realized that God had allowed them in order that the gospel might be spread more effectively (Phil 1:12).

If there is failure, a health problem, trouble in the church or house group, we can maintain a right perspective by continuing our quiet times as a means of staying close to the God who loves us and who knows all. Yet I can hear some of you saying: 'You don't really understand my situation, writing from behind a comfortable college principal's desk!' It's true, I don't know precisely what it's like to be in your shoes, but I do know, from the personal crises through which I've passed, that the worst thing you can do is to turn your back on God. The right path to take is doggedly to cling to God. Only then will we really discover how good he is.

More effective service

It's possible to be very energetic and productive in working for God, even with a stale devotional life. I've proved that for the first nineteen years of my Christian life. But there is a world of difference between success brought about largely by human endeavour and the effectiveness of service which springs from a deepening knowledge of God. Once our quiet times have become a 'built in' part of our lives rather than a tiresome addition, there will be a special input from God in all that we do for him. Sometimes it happens quite spontaneously without our knowledge, because it's 'normal' for God's influence to operate in our ministry. At other times we are very conscious of his intervention and help.

We mistakenly tend to glamorize some kinds of work for God, especially ministry from the pulpit. Because we regard such service as more vital than other aspects of leadership, it's easy to feel that only a special category of people need to stay close to God, because of the 'importance' of *their* work. This can lead to slackness on our part, because we don't consider our ministry to be of sufficient value to merit the effort.

Every Christian has been given at least one spiritual gift for use in building up others. Even those whose ministry is low-key and apparently mundane need God's power if they are to help people to grow effectively. Such work will be greatly enhanced if we stay close to the one from whom our gifts come.

There are many areas of rather more public ministry, where we may not have recognized the need for God's special inspiration. Peter writes, 'If anyone speaks, he should do it as one speaking the very words of God' (1 Pet 4:11). Whenever we speak to people, whether in one-to-one counselling, Sunday School teaching, house-group leadership or youth ministry, they have a right to hear God's voice through us so that they will grow. We can acquire valuable expertise through training, advice, practice and reading; but it will not guarantee that we will be channels of God's power, love and wisdom. It isn't enough just to do a good job. Those who habitually spend time with God each day are more likely to speak his words when they counsel someone, teach a class or lead a Bible study.

Some of us do address larger groups of people and have a special responsibility to bring not merely a 'correct' message, but one which is inspired by God. We can then expect it to bear fruit. We will not all be prophets, yet

our words ought to penetrate hearts 'prophetically'—
that is, they should be timely, appropriate, challenging
and edifying. Those who have learned to listen to God
each day, and to know his involvement in their moment
by moment living, will be able to speak the 'words of
God'.

A place of springs

We have already referred to the disaster of the vicious
downward spiral of dry devotional times and all-day dryness. The opposite, a victorious upward spiral, can be
brought about by many things like obedience and hard
work. But it is especially linked to the devotional life.
The writer of Psalm 84 discovered that those who focus
on closeness and trust in God can pass through the driest
desert (like the barren valley of Baca in verse 6) and can
make it a 'place of springs' (v. 6). Spiritually 'they go
from strength to strength' (v. 7).

Our devotional lives provide the key to releasing those
refreshing streams into our own lives. Like those canals
in Pakistan making the desert villages green, so we become channels of God's love and power to parched lives
around us. And that's what leadership is all about.

4

What Motivates Me?

'All behaviour is motivated. All behaviour makes sense,' wrote Lawrence Crabb, a Christian counsellor.[1] A perfect leader will be motivated to lead in a manner governed by his God-given basic temperament, his spiritual gifts, the nature of the church situation and the kind of people he's leading. He will know how they tick and will be able to work out the best way to help them to grow spiritually. In other words, the way he does things shows that he is the kind of person whose main aim is to meet other people's needs. His concern is for the individual or the group for which he is responsible, rather than for himself. He will have a high degree of objectivity in who should be trained to work alongside him, when to dig his heels in, and when to give in.

Unfortunately most of us are not like that. Our leadership styles, relationships, inward and outward reactions are not completely governed by that which would benefit others, but by our own emotional needs. The driving force of our inner motivation is towards ourselves. The pressures caused by our emotional needs often control how we do things. The resulting leadership style may be

---

[1]Lawrence S. Crabb Jr, *Effective Biblical Counselling* (Zondervan), p. 76.

totally the opposite of what would help people to grow.

You may have heard a description of weak leadership: 'The bland leading the bland.' Why would a particular leader choose to lead like that? In a word—fear. Fear of unpopularity caused by taking a firmer hand. Such a person feels that his need to be liked might be denied, so he protects himself by doing nothing which might upset people. Why is another leader totally authoritarian— everyone must do what he says? Maybe it's his low self-esteem that drives him to prevent anyone else from taking a leadership position—he *needs* that power in order to feel good about his personal worth.

The fact that personal needs create pressure on us to fulfil them is not in the least wrong. It is quite normal, because we're human. At the most basic level there is a need for physical survival. Thirst, hunger, and being too hot or too cold motivate us to drink, eat, and remove or put on clothes. Unless there is a severe drought or famine, fulfilling those particular needs doesn't normally rob anyone else—so the fact that our motivation is towards ourselves isn't a great problem.

Emotional needs are in a different league altogether. We often attempt to meet them at the expense of those we lead. Unfortunately we do this without even being aware of it and we harm people without ever intending to do so. The man who rules with an iron rod is subconsciously bolstering his self-esteem. What he is really saying within himself is 'I will feel better about my self-worth if I can maintain control over others.'

There are several ways of listing our emotional needs, but broadly speaking they come under such headings as self-esteem, security in relationships, and being recognized as a 'somebody' whose existence makes an impact on others. Because human beings (even Christians) are essentially self-centred, we give our own needs high priority. It is easy to fall into the trap of manipulating others to satisfy ourselves. That is why the biblical practice of self-denial is so difficult—it's not natural.

I'm not suggesting that we each go on a witch hunt for wrong motivation because that could be unhealthy. However, I am aware that some leaders are not matching their styles to the needs of their people. This is because they are under pressure to fulfil emotional gaps, and doing so unfortunately controls how they lead.

It is worth having a look at some of the outward signs of wrong motivation (let's call them the symptoms), and the possible causes (the diseases). But beware! Read what follows as you would a medical book—otherwise you could frighten yourself into thinking you're doing everything for the wrong reasons—and consequently give up altogether! The good news is that we have a God who provides the remedies (the medicine or surgery) so that our leadership will be genuinely self-less—looking after the needs of others rather than our own.

Relationship needs

Keeping in with people

Sometimes it can be lonely being the person in charge. That sense of isolation can make us hurt inside. It is often very tempting to find ways of protecting ourselves because the fundamental need to be loved and accepted often seems to be denied. Keeping in with people offers the opportunity for them to meet that need to be loved. Doing or saying things which are unpopular (which we sometimes have to do) often results in negative reactions towards us. Some of us can't cope with that, so we avoid the pain of being disliked at the expense of firm leadership.

Because I'm a sensitive person I have made many mistakes in order to guarantee a constant supply of love and encouragement in my direction. Time and time again I have failed to provide positive leadership in case people disliked me. My sermons too were what I believed they wanted to hear, so that I could not be criticized and made to feel rejected. Today I do speak what I think God has given me to say—yet I still manipulate people into saying how well I have preached.

Occasionally God calls upon us to take a tough route, and the price is unpopularity. When the going is hard it is tempting to persuade people to provide support using the 'poor me' technique which results from inner self-pity. Some of us surround ourselves with a small group of backslappers who boost our self-esteem, which can take a battering when we follow God's way. There is a danger of becoming too dependent on such people. Sometimes we avoid unpopularity altogether by making decisions they'll like, or failing to rebuke when it's needed.

One of my biggest problems resulting from my need to be liked is that I used to make myself too available to people. I wanted to be loved and respected as a person who cared. I always put their needs first before my own, however inconvenient it was. Sounds commendable, doesn't it! Unfortunately my motivation was decidedly suspect. I cared about me more than them. I nearly wore myself out with my 'come to my study whenever you choose and stay as long as you like' policy. Then there was the problem of guilt. I couldn't rest easy unless I had seen everyone who said he or she needed me. Occasionally I used to hear criticism that I didn't give enough time to the students. Despite the cost, I had to ensure that I was liked and so I redoubled my efforts.

I haven't completely solved the problem, but I'm working on it. I haven't become a big ogre, nor do I often pin a 'busy' sign on my door, but I make myself much less available. I still struggle inwardly, but I have learned to say, 'I'm very sorry, but I really can't see you this week,' or, if I'm not his or her personal tutor, 'Is it something your own tutor could help you with?'

For those who are highly motivated by the need to be liked there is a strong internal pressure to conform to what other people expect. There is nothing wrong in trying to avoid unnecessary offence. Leaders do have to conform more than most people. But we must not allow people's expectations to dominate us through fear. To do so is to lose our own freedom and identity. What is even more important is that we may fail to do what God wants us to for fear of upsetting people, and consequently we step outside his will—a high price for meeting a need.

For those with a poor self-image, criticism is particularly hard to handle. Some criticism is inevitable if we are doing our work properly. We must remember that we're in the business of helping people to become mature and Christ-like, rather than merely making them feel good— and some of them won't thank us for it! The result of meeting the need to be always liked is that we may fail to assist them towards maturity, because meeting our own need comes first.

Fighting shy of people

For various reasons, some people react in the opposite way—they are not dependent on other people's love and acceptance. They tend to steer clear of close relationships. Because all behaviour is motivated, this meets a need too—to prevent them from being hurt. They provide protection by making themselves less vulnerable, because they probably made up their minds years ago that if you get close to people they can smash you.

So what's wrong with feeling more comfortable at a distance? The answer is that the people we lead will be robbed because our behaviour is self-centred—our protection matters more than their needs. Leaders who are like this often make tasks and projects a higher priority than relationships. Some people I know are just like machines—efficient and productive, but as persons unapproachable, or adopting an air of busyness. Unfortunately it isn't good enough to relate to people just on a task level, because leadership is more about people than work. And people need our friendship and love.

I have been surprised to find that some leaders simply do not know how to love people. They may be skilled in administration or teaching, yet they lack the most important quality of all. Somewhere from the past or the present lurks the reason. Maybe they fear that love will be rejected, and that would violate the need to know that love has been accepted. Maybe their inner resources are insufficient because too little love has been received over the years—they are far too empty inside for any love to overflow to others.

You can't be an effective leader without achieving a certain level of closeness to people. Jesus wanted his disciples to be with him (Mk 3:14) because equipping others is based on relationships, not a set of detailed instructions. Closeness brings about exposure of our real selves. If a leader is afraid that people might see his faults, he may keep people at arm's length, for fear of rejection if his weaknesses are discovered.

The need to be somebody

At a function in aid of the mentally handicapped my wife was asked a strange question: 'Excuse me—but are you somebody?' What the questioner wanted to know was whether she was a person of importance in the organization.

If we have an overwhelming desire to be a 'somebody' then we shall focus more on that than on serving others —making *them* into somebodies. Our motivation will be towards ourselves and our own reputation. There are two ways of achieving this—both of them are wrong. One is to push other people down. The other is to lift ourselves to an exalted position to be admired by all.

Keeping them down

Theoretically at least, we believe in the truth that every Christian has at least one spiritual gift for use in building up the local body of Christ.

We would also acknowledge that the task of leaders is first to help people recognize what their gifts are, second to help them develop those gifts, and third, to use their abilities in an appropriate sphere of service. Christian management books use the term 'delegation', but I prefer the more biblical concept of 'equipping' others to serve actively somewhere within the local church. This is a vital aspect of all leadership work whether you're a minister, youth leader, house-group leader or a PCC member. If for any reason we fail to carry out these steps we are hindering the growth of individuals and of the congregation.

Sounds simple, doesn't it? However, there are snags. You may be the minister of a church which expects you to have all the gifts and do all the work. Your efforts to draw others into leadership and service may be thwarted. Your youth group or women's fellowship may not be very committed to serving God and will be quite apathetic towards their gifts being discovered. You'll never win with some people because they fear doing anything at all —they think they'll do it badly and get criticized for it.

By far the biggest hold-up is often the leader himself or herself. Yes, it could be you! To equip and mobilize some people will pose no threat to us at all, and we will be highly motivated to help them achieve God's goals in their lives. However, there are usually several people in the group for which we are responsible who could outshine us if they developed their full potential. This might attract attention away from us. Even worse, they may eventually replace us. If personal prestige means more to us than the development of others, then we will not be inclined to help them grow. Although it is a lie, it is very easy to feel that our real worth depends on our staying at the top of the pile. If we were to lose that position our self-esteem would drop, causing us pain. So we hinder the development of others to fit in with our mistaken idea that personal worth depends on being top dog.

In one area of Africa some of the missionaries refused to show the black Africans how to do things because they knew they themselves would eventually have no work left to do. In the same region, the black pastors were afraid of bright church members and refused to train them for Christian service. Fortunately the former problem is now less of a problem—most societies are aiming to work themselves out of a job in order to begin new work elsewhere.

If God gives us a position of so-called power, then we should accept it, and with humility use it for the good of others. We must be sure that the power has come from God. An indication that it is God-given is when the power seeks the leader rather than vice versa. This is true of all spiritual gifts and positions in church—it is the work which should seek the person with the gift rather than the other way round.

I have noticed that some leaders seem compelled to dominate people. Often they have a poor self-image and keeping people dependent boosts their sense of personal importance. I think that some of them feel rather inadequate. Others may not be so competent as leaders. A display of authority could be a cover-up for either.

Domination may be on a one-to-one level, as a member of a committee or even over an entire congregation. I tend to feel rather uncomfortable when a person takes it upon himself to determine God's will for other people. I fear that their real reason is to maintain control over people's lives. And there is no more powerful way of doing this than to claim 'thus saith the Lord'. I am not trying to run down those who have a God-given gift of perception in relation to other people. What I am concerned about is when power is used in a way which is condemned in 1 Peter 5.

The suggestion of infallibility is used commonly today. When that is the case people find it difficult to resist the commands given, because a reply is often couched in emotive theological terms: 'How dare you challenge what God has said?'

Let me suggest an acid test to see how much value you place on the possession of power. How do you react when someone else is 'promoted' or praised? Do you feel a sense or rivalry? Or are you glad they can be used by God in a wider way? Paul writes in Philippians 2:3-4: 'Do nothing out of selfish ambition or vain conceit, but in humility consider others better than yourselves. Each of you should look not only to your own interests, but also to the interests of others.' Jealousy is a sure sign that you are more concerned for yourself.

Elevating me

It's quite natural for us to want to be noticed and admired. But how strong is that need in you and me? To what extent do we give in to it? How will that affect our leadership?

Have you ever had the desire to be nationally famous? Well, possibly no more than a few mild fantasies. Probably quite harmless. But on a smaller scale, coveting public recognition can distract us from the true essence of leadership, namely servanthood. Those who haven't got the opportunity for wide public recognition in church may self righteously say 'tut-tut' to those seeking prominence among the whole congregation. Yet in principle they may still do the same whether it's within a house group or a small cluster of friends chatting after the service. Seeking position blinds us to the feelings of other people, because we are using them to meet our own needs rather than vice versa.

How about name dropping? Do you do it? Why? To impress! I did it quite recently with a non-Christian neighbour who wanted to know if Leighton Ford was worth hearing. 'Oh yes,' I replied, 'I've known him since 1961. In fact, I was with him just a few weeks ago in Wales. His son went to the same university as I did in the USA . . . bla . . . bla . . . bla . . .!

When our emphasis is on status or position, then being a leader in the style of the New Testament will be difficult. Position can lead to pride, and pride seeks praise rather than concerning itself with the growth and fulfilment of other people. It is essentially self-centred.

Cultivating an image can be a major pre-occupation for some. What it does is to channel our energies away from others and towards ourselves. Subconsciously our thinking goes something like this: 'I need to feel a worthwhile person. If other people will admire me then I'll achieve that aim. They'll only admire me if they see that I have "charisma", or that everything I do is successful.' But this thinking is wrong. We are already worthwhile— God made us and he says we have worth.

In New Testament times, the Scribes and Pharisees were very image-conscious. Read Matthew 23:1-12 and you'll see what I mean. They liked to be greeted in the public places and to be offered places of honour at banquets. They prided themselves in teaching people the truth, yet in practice they laid heavy burdens on them. It is significant that they were so pre-occupied with themselves that they were not 'willing to lift a finger' to help those in need (v.4). When they fasted they wanted everyone to know of their dedication to God by making it obvious that they hadn't eaten. As Jesus rightly commented: 'Everything they do is done for men to see' (v. 5). It was against such image-building and hypocrisy that Jesus pronounced his seven woes.

Anyone who is over concerned with position will find it hard to serve others. They are mutually exclusive. Focusing on being the centre of attention blinds us to the needs of others.

One of the severest jolts I ever had was when I arrived to take over the leadership of Moorlands. In my mind I saw myself as a famous national leader—invitations to preach at places like All Souls and Lansdowne Baptist Church would pour in. In fact no such offers came, and the real situation was nothing less than humiliating. I found myself rodding out the sewers, climbing into the slimy cesspit, reroofing the buildings and mending the lawnmower.

It takes hard work to maintain an image—you have to constantly remind people that you are superior to ordinary men and women. For example, while others might take a day off work to redecorate the lounge, an image-builder does not want other people to know that he is more or less the same as they are—so he tells them he's 'working at home today', and goes off with a big briefcase full of papers. Ordinary mortals might occasionally arrive late for work, but no such ordinary explanation will do for him—he is not late for work, he 'has been delayed'. And while others simply read the paper, he would prefer to describe his activity as 'keeping himself informed'.

How much do you cultivate an image? Dare you ask a few close friends what they really feel about you? Are you content for the real you to show through, or are you trying to make people see someone different.

The medicine

Anyone who suggests that leadership is a peaceful bed of roses ought to have his head examined! Like Alice in Wonderland who had to believe seven impossible things before breakfast, we sometimes have to do two opposite things at the same time, and that causes tension.

Sometimes that feeling of anxiety cannot be resolved and we simply have to live with it, because it goes with the job. We recognize that it is part of the price we have to pay. At one and the same time we are under pressure to fulfil our own needs and to supply others. It's impossible to do both simultaneously. We need to identify with people and get close to them, yet at the same time we have to remain slightly detached and isolated from the group we lead. Men and women like me have a strong need to be with people who provide love and acceptance, and yet I know that sometimes we have to survive alone —and it hurts.

It is highly unlikely that we will be able totally to avoid all forms of attack or deprivation of our needs. As we have already seen we could enjoy a reasonably peaceful life but at the expense of other people's growth, by exercising the wrong kind of leadership. To do what is right will always cause us some pain because a competition exists between meeting their needs and mine. To look after theirs may mean neglecting my own.

I fully believe that the tension many of us experience need not be quite so acute. This is true especially where leaders' needs are so pressing that they are preoccupied with receiving rather than giving—thus spoiling their work of building up people. There is a need to escape from that deficit cycle in order to work more positively for the benefit of others.

The advantages of such a change are enormous. The leader benefits from a reduction in tension, and the group he or she leads gets what it deserves.

For instance, once a way has been found to cope with the self-esteem problem, we can entrust others with responsibility—they no longer threaten us. Ultimately they may outshine us and we should be able to rejoice in it. If we can reduce the pressures created by the need to be liked we will waste less time worrying about their reactions to what we do or say. Having to maintain an image takes constant hard work and is fraught with anxiety. If we could be free from having to do this then we shouldn't need to spend so much time proving how good we are. It would release us from having to maintain that fragile facade. Instead, people could see us as we really are.

God can meet that deficit

Is there really any viable alternative to having our emotional needs met totally by the people around us? The answer has to be 'yes'. What is the point of being a Christian if we have no more resources than unbelievers? Since our God is a personal God he is able to provide an escape route from our deficit cycle.

God often chooses to meet our needs through other people, whether they are emotional or spiritual. He also does it personally and directly. He provides security ('Who shall separate us from the love of Christ?' Rom 8:35), and he ensures that we are somebodies by giving us important work to do ('For we are God's workmanship, created in Christ Jesus to do good works' Eph 2:10). Even if all our needs were denied by the people around us, we could survive because our real security lies in our relationship with God and that cannot be destroyed. As for being a somebody, there is no better person than God with whom to be a somebody. If *he* says I'm important then I can walk ten feet tall among those I lead, however badly they may treat me. I remain a somebody for ever. Other people's admiration is pleasant but not essential.

My value as a person does not actually depend on other people liking me or putting me on a pedestal (even though my emotions may say that it does). The whole issue of my worth has already been settled—God made me, he loves me, and he has declared me to be special.

When Paul, Silas and Timothy were under attack by some of the Thessalonians, they felt a sense of disapproval. It hurt them deeply and they could easily have become men-pleasers rather than obeying God—thus reducing the pain. Fortunately, Paul remembered that the only approval which really mattered was God's. 'We speak as men approved by God' (1 Thess 2:4). His need for approval was met by God as a result of doing what was right, rather than from men as a reward for pleasing them. Despite the denial of significance from other people, he remained selfless because God had provided the necessary emotional input. What really counts is not what people think of our Christian service but what God thinks about it (2 Cor 10:12-18). Once we know with certainty that God is pleased with us, then we can survive, even when we feel anxious about it.

The extent to which we will be able to draw on divine resources will depend on the depth of our relationship with God. We need to know him well enough that when we feel threatened and are tempted to handle things wrongly, we will turn to God to take care of our emotional needs. The stronger our devotional lines, the more easily we shall be able to draw on his resources. The more we accept that we already possess all we need in God, the less we will seek it from others—and that will result in a New Testament style leadership.

Even so, there is still a price to pay

Leadership usually carries with it the enormous satisfaction of seeing people grow. We warmly welcome this aspect of our work. What we don't look for is the price we may have to pay in order to do what God asks.

We have already seen that the pressure to meet our own needs can be eased considerably through our relationship with God. But it doesn't mean that we are immune to feeling rejected or threatened, because we are still human. The only way to avoid that would be to behave self-centredly by finding ways to protect ourselves—resulting in poor leadership.

We have two alternatives. We could choose to reduce personal anxiety by focusing on our own needs, but our followers would pay the price of being badly led. We could decide to look after other people. In that case *we* would pay the price. Someone has to make the sacrifice. Whenever there is a competition between their needs and ours, and we let theirs win, we will experience anxiety. When we follow God's way our emotions could take quite a battering. Like Paul's thorn in the flesh, no matter how hard we pray the problem isn't going to go away. We simply have to put up with it. Occasionally you have to stand alone, as Paul once did when only the Lord Jesus provided support (2 Tim 4:16 f.).

Popularity may be quite easy to achieve, but it is usually achieved only by compromising. It is better to focus on gaining respect, but that will cause us some pain.

To be effective we must get close to people. For some that can be threatening and very costly. To be an open and honest person is so unfamiliar that fear of it often drives some leaders to play safe and avoid the cost.

To encourage others to develop can take great courage in some situations. But it has to be done. No one can exercise true leadership unless he can genuinely take pleasure in the success of others. So regardless of our own feelings we must seek to select and train people for appropriate spheres of service.

Some people hardly lead at all because it's safer that way. It takes real guts to act more positively, because inevitably some people will dislike what they are doing. Conversely, those who protect themselves by being auto-crats will suffer considerable anxiety as they adjust to a more biblical and selfless leadership style.

People's expectations of us can be a real nuisance. Unfortunately we cannot escape from certain aspects of this—it comes with the job. One or two people will put us on pedestals, and maintaining the image they project onto us can be difficult. They expect so much of us that they are shattered when the slightest imperfection shows through. They don't like to think of us as normal human beings. They try to impose detailed restrictions and re-quirements on our lives—ones they would never dream of applying to themselves. Some of us would love to say 'rhubarb' to them and to be more free in our behaviour, but they won't *let* us. Perhaps the best answer is to go at least twenty miles away and do our own thing! (I'm quite serious about this.)

One or two in our group will treat us as slaves—they expect us to be available night and day. ('Oh I do hope you won't mind my ringing you at 12.30 a.m. but I really needed to chat.') There does come a time when we have to call a halt with some people for the sake of our own sanity and maintaining right priorities. The price? Guilt feelings!

How did Jesus cope? Through prayer and obedience he experientially found his security and significance in his heavenly Father. At the same time we must remember that he was fully human and therefore he too paid a price for his leadership. Whatever the personal cost (and often it was high), he always led in a way which would bring maximum benefit for his disciples. Although he was a receiver as well as a giver, his own work as a leader was not dependent on love and friendship being offered to him. When his disciples failed him in Gethsemane he was very disappointed; yet he continued to do God's will.

Surprisingly, genuine authority comes to those who submit. 'Humble yourselves before the Lord and he will lift you up' (Jas 4:10). You'd expect it to be the other way round. It takes courage to submit. The question is: 'Am I strong enough to be a servant, or must I be an autocrat?' Scripture says that God 'opposes the proud' (1 Pet 5:5, quoting Prov 3:34). When the disciples argued over which of them would be the greatest, Jesus said: 'For he who is least among you all—he is the greatest' (Lk 9:48).

Am I a leader?

It is quite possible that some of us are in the wrong position—either we shouldn't be leading at all, or we ought to be in some other sphere. The 'Peter Principle' applies even in churches—namely that we get promoted from one level to another until we reach the level of our own incompetence. We need to be sure that it *is* God who has called us to lead, otherwise we may lack the motivation to keep going when things get tough. I know leaders who can't face up to the fact that they should be doing something else more appropriate to their gifts.

Before you hand in your resignation, let me add that a feeling of inadequacy is in itself not a good reason to quit! We may need to seek help of some kind, but on its own that doesn't constitute a call from God to give up. Some of the greatest leaders of all time have felt unable to do what God wanted. Moses was one of them. What did God say? 'Go and do something easier?' No, he provided a special encouragement by promising that he would be with him. He told Gideon the same. Jeremiah too felt inadequate.

God isn't looking only for people who feel sufficient —he often takes just the opposite kind of people. 'Our competence comes from God' (2 Cor 3:5). I'm definitely one of those. Humanly speaking, I'm far too sensitive for the cut and thrust of some of the situations I face.

Perhaps one of the most powerful examples of an inadequate leader is the young man Timothy. Paul had to urge him to stay at Ephesus and face the opposition of tough opponents, because that's what God had called him to do. I would never have chosen that sensitive and timid man to cope with that situation—especially as he appeared to have personality and temperament weaknesses.

If God could use men like Timothy, he can use you and me. As with Moses and so many others, he provides his strength, his equipping and his presence in all we do for him, however incapable we may feel.

Part 3

THE PROCESS OF LEADERSHIP

What style of leadership should you adopt?
What is the New Testament teaching?
What did Jesus teach?

Leadership involves teams. There is a
right way and a wrong way of working
together. Team leaders need each other,
and will only work effectively when they
have concentrated on affirming and enriching each other.

Those we lead are volunteers. They can
walk out at any time. We must use biblical
and appropriate ways of encouraging them
to grow and to serve God.

God's principles and purposes never
change, but his ways of fulfilling them do.
Our responsibility is to guide those we
lead towards hitherto unexplored ways of
living, worshipping and serving.

5
Leadership Style

The day before I flew to Delhi in September 1983 I slipped into a morning service near the airport. It was held in a rather plain community hall. The two hour gathering was very informal and there seemed to be several leaders dressed in ordinary clothing. None of them appeared to dominate each other or the congregation.

Four weeks later I found myself in the middle of the Sind desert of Pakistan. After catching the bus from Karachi to Hyderabad I took a rickshaw to the Anglican compound. As we rattled in through the main gates, a church service was obviously in progress. To my surprise, the sights and sounds were not at all what I expected in rural Pakistan. The singing was very formal and conservatively Western. The minister was obviously very much in charge and wore splendid robes rather than local Asian dress.

'Which pattern is biblical?' I asked myself. Should a church have one minister, or many? Should leadership carry a lot of authority, or very little? What should the building be like—ornate like the one in Hyderabad, or plain? And should leaders wear special uniforms as a symbol of their authority?

When it comes to leadership style and structure the variety is truly amazing—you'd think that each church had a different Bible from which it got its teaching!

Some leaders are powerfully authoritarian, whether they work as a team or alone. At the other end of the spectrum there are low-key leaders. On the whole, those churches whose leaders are weak, and who lack creative imagination, show little vision and appear not to be growing numerically or progressing spiritually. But where leaders are positive, confident and even authoritarian there is movement and growth. Also there tends to be a much higher level of personal commitment by members of the congregation.

Decision-making and the use of authority come in all shapes and sizes. Some churches are very democratic and each person is permitted his or her say in virtually everything. But there are those where the average member has little opportunity for genuine input—decisions are simply announced. More recently, churches with 'pyramid' structures provide a system in which each person has someone to whom he or she may turn, even for personal decisons like where to live, what job to take and whom to marry. Terms like shepherding and covering are currently used to describe it. And some churches don't belong to any one clean-cut category, but fall somewhere in between.

Such a variety of interpretations raises several awkward questions. Most puzzling is the fact that each church or denomination genuinely believes that it can support its practices using the Bible as the ultimate authority. Does the Bible therefore not lay down any guidelines concerning leadership style and church government? If not, then everyone is right! Or is its teaching broad enough to be interpreted in several ways, depending on the local situation? Even so, it doesn't seem possible that two contradictions can be true at the same time. Like the difference between church members having some say in what goes on, and members simply being told of a decision. Or the enormous distinction between a one-man band and team leadership.

Suppose we began with Scripture alone, and, without reference to what we are doing today, tried to discover what the Bible really says. Would we then find ourselves like the Pentecostals, Brethren, Baptists, Methodists, Anglicans, house churches? Or like none of these?

Today's styles

Before embarking on a study of biblical teaching, let us see how leaders do things today. I am not the first one to try to do this. Most books on leadership attempt to classify the various styles so that readers can identify their own way of doing things. Each author uses a different set of words to describe the various approaches. Although the majority have four, five or six categories, I am limiting my list to three—not because I want to be different, but because the ones I have chosen reflect just three broad leadership concepts.

First, those who like working in teams; second, those who do not; third, leaders who hardly lead at all.

People persons

Those who tend towards this style usually enjoy being with other people and put a high priority on relationships. They are 'people persons'. In pairs or in groups they are prepared to be open and share their lives. The apostle Paul and his assistant Timothy were like this. It is noticeable that Paul felt acute loneliness in the absence of his friends, and especially when separated from Timothy. Even in a position of authority in Thessalonica, close relationships mattered as much as the shared task of preaching the gospel.

The priority of people over work is a strong characteristic of this style. Although the tasks being done are not

unimportant, the relationships between those accompli-
shing them are a vital foundation for the success of the
work itself. If anything, the people mean more than the
achievement of goals. This leader's concern for people
rather than projects means that he considers the needs
and feelings of his co-workers as important as the getting
of results.

Goals are not neglected, but they tend to be group
goals rather than those personally selected by the leader
and imposed on the team. His whole approach to decision
making is to involve the group in plenty of discussion,
especially the informal chatty kind. He finds this quite
easy because he views his co-workers more as friends
than merely as people who obey his orders.

On the whole, his planning is thorough and tidy—
there is an atmosphere of quiet orderliness. This doesn't
mean that differences of opinion are stifled—they aren't,
because he is not threatened by them and is happy for
everyone to have his or her say. We'll say more about
this in a later chapter. The word 'democratic' might be
appropriate to describe his attitude to the involvement of
others.

Loners

Terms like 'bureaucratic', 'autocratic', and 'dynamic
achiever' describe three different styles, but they have
one thing in common—they refer to those who are not
team people.

A 'bureaucrat' is a man or woman who believes that if
you set up the right rules, regulations and procedures, all
will run smoothly. People and their personal needs are
not considered terribly important. If success and productivity were the only things that mattered in the kingdom,
then this style might have *some* merit. However, a system
which ignores the fact that you are dealing with people
will eventually fail to achieve its aims.

It is true that rules and guidelines *are* necessary when groups of people work together. But a pre-occupation with minutiae or over-fussy constitutional matters can be unhealthy. It can mean that such a leader will have difficulty in acknowledging the humanity of his colleagues, or even that he may find himself uneasy in relationships.

An 'autocrat' directs people, rather than acting as a guide and an encourager. He is more of a commander. He usually likes his ideas to be tried out first and will try to control other people's work in line with his own thinking. I rather suspect that he is threatened by ideas initiated by other people, and feels far more secure when he is in complete control. When he does work in a team, he often gains consent by manipulating people rather than freely allowing a consensus to develop. Given the opportunity he would rather answer to nobody. (Except God of course. And all too often he gets his way by hiding behind a smokescreen of 'God has revealed to me . . . .') He often moves ahead without carefully considering other people's feelings.

In contrast with a 'people person', he is more concerned with achievement of goals than with team relationships. Like an unenlightened industrial manager, he cares more about getting things done than enriching the lives of his fellow-workers.

Is this leader strong or weak? He may look extremely strong, but some are pathetically weak underneath, like a bully in a school playground. Weak ego, personality defects—on the outside very tough; but inside, very insecure.

It is worth commenting on the 'dynamic achiever', because he really is different from the bureaucrat or autocrat. Because he is so full of drive and energy he wants to be where the action is. He is not normally a detailed and careful planner. He delegates a huge amount of authority because he has confidence in the people he leads. I once worked alongside a professor like that. He used to come into the laboratory about once every three weeks, throw a lot of ideas at us to try out, and then disappear until the next time.

The non-leader

Far from wanting public prominence, this leader is happier receeding into the background. He would prefer to let things run their natural course. He would not normally place demands on people, unlike his autocratic counterpart. Perhaps he feels that if everything is running quietly, why interfere? Or he might think that focusing on the leader is not a good thing.

For this leader, people are definitely a priority over goals, but his strongest motivation is towards creating a quiet life for himself. He may see normal internal stress as unspiritual; so nothing is done to disturb the status quo. He just takes things as they come, and if little is achieved he is not particularly concerned.

Is this leader secure or insecure? He may be strong and secure, genuinely not worrying about what others think about his leadership, or whether anything is achieved or not. His desire for a quiet life and his failure to give direction to the people he is responsible for could be the consequence of fear concerning the hassles that inevitably come to those who take a real lead.

Boss or head

If we are to lead in a biblical manner, we must understand the nature of the group we lead, whether we are responsible for an entire congregation or just a small group, a miniature 'church'. We also need to know how that group relates to Christ, how it grows, and where we as leaders fit into the picture.

First and foremost the church is a living body, not an earthly organization or institution. We must therefore

view our own group in that way because it will ensure
that we lead in the right way. God's purpose is that the
church should grow spiritually and achieve certain aims,
such as evangelism. Internal growth depends on the loving
and healthy interaction of all the various members of the
church. The Spirit supplies the gifts to equip each Christian
to play his or her part in building up others. Therefore
one of the aims of leadership is to assist that healthy
functioning. To do that we must show people how to
relate more deeply to the Spirit and to help them discover
their gifts.

However, if we view the group or church as an organization (or even worse as *my* church, *my* house group,
my youth team) then we are quite likely to see ourselves
as its managers, and could easily use a management or
authoritarian approach. The result of this is that we will
hinder the relationship to their real leader, Christ the
Head of the body, because we are placing ourselves as
earthly bosses over them—thus directing their attention
to our wishes not Christ's.

In this sense of 'leadership', not even Christ wants to
be a 'boss' to people. As Lord we obey him. But we also
relate to him as Head and as such, he is the supplier of
strength, power, encouragement and enabling—because
he is our source of life. He is also the co-ordinator of the
parts of the body so that the whole of it grows.

The concept of headship is used by Paul when referring
to marriage in Ephesians 5:21–38. He sees the marriage
relationship not as one of command and obedience focusing on the authority of the husband, but on the husband
nourishing and supporting the wife he loves.

This is the kind of leadership that we must imitate in
our work. It is care rather than control. It is serving the
people, as opposed to demanding obedience. It is directing
them to the supreme Head, so that they grow up into
him not us (Eph 4:15).

So far from being managers, we are servants. At the same time, leaders are responsible for the quality of congregational life and to some extent for personal growth. It is our privilege to exercise that responsibility in an appropriate style.

How not to lead

It may seem strange to include some information on how *not* to do something! However, better writers than I have set the precedent, and it can be helpful to be aware of dangers and pitfalls. For example, Richards and Hoeldtke in their book *A Theology of Church Leadership* have a section entitled '12 ways to dominate instead of leading' —very enlightening!

Some of today's definitions of leadership can give the wrong impression of what the church is and what the biblical function of a leader ought to be. They focus primarily on the tasks to be done, rather than the growth of the individual. They imply that the people we care for constitute nothing more than an organization producing results, and that with good management techniques the aims will be achieved.

Please don't get me wrong. I'm not saying that these terms are always inappropriate. In fact I teach Christian management and leadership to potential pastors, evangelists and missionaries training at Moorlands Bible College. I unashamedly use terminology like 'planning', 'leading', 'organizing', 'controlling', 'job description' and 'delegation'.

A good deal of Christian work does involve management and producing results. For those involved in such ministries, these concepts are perfectly valid. Organizations like Scripture Union and missionary societies need competent management if they are to function smoothly. Even churches—especially larger ones—have an organizational aspect to them, and we must be good stewards of our resources whether they be people, buildings or money.

But what concerns me is that if we see our church or group as a result-producer alone, then we will neglect the main purpose of leadership—namely to help people to grow spiritually and to develop a healthy worshipping congregation. You can't deal with these things as you can the mass distribution of literature or the organizing of a city-wide crusade. It's not 'getting things done through people' we primarily need—it's building them up. Christians *are* meant to achieve things like evangelizing the lost, but these activities should come as a result of growth, not instead of it.

So let us avoid seeing people primarily as workers who exist to carry out plans, but rather as those whose main aim is to mature.

Power

Power corrupts. Absolute power corrupts absolutely. Can this apply to Christians serving God? Yes, in a way it can. Sadly two of the disciples, together with their mother, fell into this temptation by asking for a position of authority in Jesus' kingdom (Mt 20:20). This gave Jesus the opportunity to talk about real leadership—not being preoccupied with authority but servanthood. 'Whoever wants to become great among you must be your servant, and whoever wants to be first must be your slave—just as the Son of man did not come to be served, but to serve, and to give his life as a ransom for many' (vv. 26–28). Similarly, when the disciples had argued among themselves about who was the greatest, Jesus again taught humility and servanthood (Mk 9:33–37). Jesus was soon to live out his own teaching by becoming the ultimate servant.

Provided we see the power and authority of the positions

we hold in church as something held in trust and a tool
for building people up, then all is well. Unfortunately
some leaders who have started out with the right attitude
have allowed it steadily to degenerate until they believe
they own the power, and hence want to increase it. You
don't have to be pastor over 200 people to slip in this
way. You could be the leader of only eight in a house
group.

To be preoccupied with power means less concern for
the needs and feelings of the people we serve. We could
end up dominating them and pushing them in directions
to suit ourselves, or to preserve our authority. It is true
that some people prefer to be controlled by a strong
leader. But is it good for them in the long run?

Covering

The word 'covering' can mean different things in different situations. It often implies that each member of a
congregation has someone available (or above them) to
whom they may (or must) turn for guidance and advice
concerning the will of God in their lives. In some churches
it can mean a high level of control, but in others it is
more a matter of advice than receiving orders.

To have someone to turn to who is wise and spiritually
mature is valuable. In my own church, those who would
like to seek advice from one or more elders may do so
voluntarily. They are under no obligation to follow the
counsel given, whether in the realm of marriage, career
or house purchase.

It is obviously useful to have leaders who are able to
protect people from making foolish or sinful decisions.
Sometimes they may need to urge people strongly to do
this or not to do that for their own good. But there is a
big difference between voluntarily asking for help, and
being in a situation where a leader effectively becomes

Jesus to other people. Thus to be at odds with the leader's wishes is to be at odds with the will of God.

To be asked to submit to Christ's indirect authority vested in a 'shepherd' (or whatever name is used) does have some advantages, but there are some real dangers. First, the leader may fall into the temptation of enjoying the use of power and thus misuse it to satisfy his own appetites. Second, because every human is fallible he could be wrong and therefore lead people in the wrong direction. Third, it could discourage people from seeking God's will in a direct relationship with Christ, and relieve them of that important responsibility. Some people easily drift into becoming dependent on a leader rather than facing the personal struggle to discover what God is saying. It could be the easy way out.

In one or two churches, leaders have steadily built up numerous rules and regulations for the lives and conduct of the congregation. Often complete conformity is expected. One has only to see the sad situation among the Exclusive Plymouth Brethren to be aware of the quicksands into which some of today's churches are slowly sinking. They are blissfully unaware that the freedom they once enjoyed is steadily turning into legalism and bureaucracy.

On the positive side, God does expect leaders to exercise oversight. They are not to sit back and let things drift. Unfortunately many in the past have failed to give a lead, and some are reluctant to do so even today. In my own church those of us who are elders are much more positive and more directive than we used to be. Today I act and speak much more boldly when people seek my help, rather than the fashionable non-directive style I had previously been using.

With what style may we assist growth?

What the New Testament says

One of the things that frightens some people about servanthood is that they think of it as servility, that you have to let people treat you like a doormat. But that's not what it's all about. Jesus was the most humble servant who ever lived, yet he never lost his dignity. What was his style? I decided to read right through the gospels to find out, so that I could adopt it too. To my surprise I found not just one style but many—each one appropriate to the situation.

Sometimes Jesus exhibited great gentleness—in the way he received young children, his healing of Mary as he held her by the hand and then helped her up, his compassion on the lepers, on the paralytic and on Jairus' daughter.

He showed great patience and concern for the disciples. When they were terrified of drowning in the storm he rebuked the wind. And just as Peter began sinking when he walked on the water, Jesus took hold of him to steady him.

Though he was the Lord, he taught and practised servanthood among his closest followers, his disciples. He washed their dirty, sweaty feet. At the last supper instead of them serving him as he had every right to be, he did the work himself. 'The greatest among you should be like the youngest, and the one who rules like the one who serves. For who is greater, the one who is at the table or the one who serves? Is it not the one who is at the table? But I am among you as one who serves' (Lk 22:26f.).

Being a servant is not the same as being weak. Jesus sharply rebuked Peter for his denial that Jesus would have to die. He complained when the disciples couldn't stay awake to support him in Gethsemane. In his denunciation of the Jewish leaders (in the passage known as the 'seven woes' in Matthew 23) he spoke strong words. His righteous anger at the salesmen and moneychangers in the temple brought about an act of strong and violent condemnation—he overthrew their tables.

The Epistles undoubtedly teach that leaders sometimes have to rebuke, command and challenge people. Yet it must be done within the framework of servanthood. The New Testament sees tenderness more than toughness and nurture more than nastiness. 'For you know that we dealt with each of you as a father deals with his children, encouraging, comforting and urging you to live lives worthy of God' (1 Thess 2:11); 'And the Lord's servant must not quarrel; instead, he must be kind to everyone, able to teach, not resentful. Those who oppose him he must gently instruct' (2 Tim 2:24f.).

It is more a question of seeking voluntary heart-commitment than of requiring obedience through coercion or manipulation. The leader is 'among' his people rather than 'over'. He shows them rather than tells them. In Acts 6, Stephen, though spiritually head and shoulders over the other six deacons, served at table along with them. In his life he demonstrated that true greatness consists of serving others. 'The greatest among you will be your servant' (Mt 23:11).

Direct them to God, not ourselves

In a sense, the only authority any of us carries is the authority to build people up by helping them to relate more closely to the Father, Son and Holy Spirit—so that they may worship the Father, respond to Christ as Lord, and develop deep fellowship with the Spirit, seeking his help in prayer, giftedness and the exalting of Christ in their lives.

We are to encourage them to live out the will of God, not *our* wills. We must equip rather than control. Whatever style we use, it must not intrude into Jesus' headship of the body, the worship of the Father, or the Spirit's role. We are primarily facilitators of others. We must help them to discover their gifts and roles where they will be fruitful in the local church.

Administration is OK

I may have given the impression that I despise good administration and that I prefer a situation where each person does his own thing as 'led by the Spirit'—nothing organized and no one in a position of prominence and authority. Not at all! But some do. They think it is boring, unnecessary, unspiritual, secular and not sacred. Those who see it as evil will put little effort into it. Often it shows!

We do need good administration. Some churches now have a full-time administrator whose specific spiritual gift this is (Rom 12:8—'If it is in leadership, let him govern diligently,'; 1 Cor 12:28—'Gifts of administration'). Why do we need it? Proverbs 11:14 sums it up: 'Where no wise administration exists, the people flounder.'

What we don't need is management for its own sake, or a form of management which treats people as production workers. What we do need is the minimum amount of administration necessary to fulfil the purpose of the church community, which is to help people grow and serve Christ more effectively. If a certain kind of management genuinely facilitates this, let's have it. If it only keeps the church humming like a piece of well-oiled machinery and people don't mature, let's get rid of it!

Most leaders have to do some administration. If this happens to be one of your personal weaknesses (you can't be good at everything) then you really do need to learn how to do it better. May I suggest reading some of the excellent books which are available today (mostly American!). If you are the pastor of a busy church and you can't cope, or it simply isn't your gift, then how about asking the rest of the leadership to select someone from the congregation, release him from his job, get him trained, and offer him full-time employment in the church?

Power can be OK

What about prominence, power and authority? Are they always wrong? No, far from it. Timothy certainly carried special responsibilities over and above the elders and deacons in Ephesus. From Acts 15 it is clear that James was the leader of the Jerusalem elders.

There is nothing wrong with offices or titles such as chairman, chairwoman, pastor, if they describe someone's function and they are doing the work for the right reasons. Our diaconate is eighteen strong and we have a permanent lay chairman who co-ordinates things. He is far more visible than the other deacons, because people in the church need to know whom to contact. Our eldership is different. We have a chairmanship which rotates once a month. We have decided that all seven elders should have a reasonably high public profile, not just the pastor.

Recognizing your style

For those inclined that way, there are questionnaires designed for self-analysis which give an indication of leadership style. We use one of them at college. Although it gives some useful information it is not completely reliable. We only partly take it seriously. We have some fun with it too. Once a husband and wife were both diagnosed as having a power complex. We all laughed and wondered how they got on in their marriage!

May I suggest that you think back over the past months and assess each of the different situations in which you have been a leader—public meetings, one-to-one conversations, and committees. Did you usually announce your decision at the outset? Did you manipulate people?

Or did you thrash things out as equals and come to a generally agreed decision? Did you set up discussion procedures? Or did you just sit back and let others worry?

More importantly, perhaps—did your style vary at all? Did you handle your diaconate as you did the stroppy youth group—by the use of strong authority? Or did you use the same approach with young converts as you did with your team of experienced open air workers, sending them out onto the streets and telling them to get on with it?

What I am questioning is whether you handle each situation differently by using the most suitable style, or whether you are locked into a single style. If that is so, then more variety and flexibility is needed. As we have seen, Jesus varied his approach enormously. There is no one correct style that suits everything.

Matching the style to the situation

Clearly some styles are never appropriate—like the use of power simply to meet the needs of the leader, or the total abdication of all leadership responsibility. Others are neither right nor wrong, but will be helpful or unhelpful depending on the circumstances. We need to be wise and sensitive enough to choose the right one each time. Sometimes a blend of more than one style is useful.

Quite a number of factors will determine what is best. A large church must be dealt with differently from a small one, or—for example—a nurture group of young believers. What are the spiritual and emotional needs of the people? Are they at a high level of maturity? A group of new Christians who in their everyday lives are unused to carrying much authority needs more direction than an eldership who come from professional backgrounds and who have been Christians for twenty years. You need a more directive style with a group of children compared to a house group.

What will most effectively help a congregation when it meets either at a service or for a discussion? Encouragement? Rebuke? Maybe just teaching so that they may draw their own conclusions? How we lead will also depend on what kind of work is being done—a group Bible study or prayer time is different from door-to-door evangelism. The age in which we live matters too. In the sixties a rather authoritarian style was acceptable but it certainly isn't today though occasionally the use of power is necessary. For example, in a crisis situation someone has got to take charge.

Whatever way we lead, if we constantly bear in mind God's goal for leadership, then we are more likely to succeed. If it directs people to Christ and his resources then the individual and those around him or her will grow—and that should be satisfaction enough for us.

'We will in all things grow up into him who is the Head, that is, Christ. From him the whole body . . . grows and builds itself up in love, as each part does its work' (Eph 4:15f.).

6

Decision-Making by the Team

During a planning meeting for Leadership '84, Lyndon Bowring suddenly blurted out: 'Why don't you just give each of us a rubber stamp, Clive?' He was speaking to Clive Calver, General Secretary of the Evangelical Alliance. The comment was a humorous one, because it appeared that Clive had already made most of the decisions before the meeting! He hadn't, of course. What he had done was a thorough piece of homework. For example, in deciding whether Rev. So-and-so should be invited to speak, it was easier to make a decision knowing in advance that if asked he would be available and willing to come.

On that occasion, we all roared with laughter. But what is less funny is when a team member actually *does* make plans and decisions before a meeting, and then announces them to his team (so-called!). Alternatively he might bully them into supporting his proposals. In theory that doesn't sound so bad because he has at least allowed a discussion, and technically a 'group' decision is made. However, the end product of the two techniques is very similar—only his wishes will be carried out.

There are other ways of misusing teams. Some of them appear to be very democratic. For example, one person's suggestions may be given wild and enthusiastic support by just one person. From the noise made by the two of them it may sound as though the whole group is in favour. Sometimes a minority may ride roughshod over the rest of the team. At the meeting, the others may seem contented; but in private there may be resentment and conflict afterwards. Similarly, the majority may override the minority. Again, there may be harmony on the surface but underneath ill feelings are generated.

It may be argued, 'But isn't that what democracy is all about—the side with the most supporters wins, and the rest have to accept that they've lost?' And what I now want to describe may at first sight look like the majority overruling the minority, but it isn't. The difference may appear subtle but it is sufficient to ensure greater team harmony and a better way of coming to a right decision.

It is called *decision-making by consensus*. What happens is this: no decision is reached until each person's opinions and feelings have been thoroughly aired. No individual, minority or even majority is allowed to bully the group into submitting to their wishes. All the issues relating to the subject under discussion are thrashed out before any conclusions can be drawn.

It takes time to develop the level of maturity for a team to work this way. Individuals have to face the fact that their ideas and suggestions may be ruggedly opposed. At first, some will feel threatened and may want to do things differently. They have to learn that a rejection of their pet idea is not a personal rejection. Team members must learn not to reject one another, even though they may sometimes be violently opposed to a particular suggestion.

This is why open, loving and trusting relationships must first be established. Without this, decision-making by consensus could be disastrous. It works best when all the group members have had the opportunity to say what they think. From the outset of the discussion there must be genuine open-mindedness—a willingness by each to have his mind changed by what others say. No one must enter the meeting with a closed mind.

The role of chairperson is very important. He or she should listen carefully to all that is said. He mustn't allow himself to dominate. Once everyone has had his say, his job is to state to the team a summary of what he thinks the group is saying. Normally there is no necessity (except in vital issues) for the group to be entirely unanimous. The consensus suggested by the chairman may not meet with everyone's 100% approval, but all present should at least be partially in agreement. Then they will be reasonably comfortable about going along with it.

Some teams take votes, others don't. It is neither right nor wrong to do so. I personally prefer not to. I would rather have a chairman who sums up what seems to be the general consensus of the team. He can tell whether he is right or not by the presence or absence of nods of approval or encouraging grunts from around the room.

We use this method at college. I usually take the chair. There is often plenty of disagreement because we are so diverse. Each of us (including myself) knows that his views may be thrown out completely.

Once the decision has been made then we all support it in public. This includes any staff member who may still totally disagree with it. His personal feelings must never emerge once the meeting is over. Disloyalty will soon destroy a team and will polarize the people for whom they are responsible. It is very dangerous for an individual to gain a following as a result of telling certain people that he was against such and such a decision.

Often the chairman has to suggest a compromise in order to accommodate as many people's views as possible. The very word 'compromise' may be abhorrent to some readers: 'Surely the whole group should be of one mind, if God has truly been speaking.' It is true that God does reveal his will in great detail sometimes, but usually he leaves some work for the team to do as well!

At Moorlands we occasionally find it impossible to arrive at a true consensus. If the matter is not urgent we may leave it twenty-four hours or even a week. Or as the Americans would say we 'sleep' on it. Often, individuals change their minds as a result of waiting and praying about it further.

Ensuring good decisions

However spiritual a leadership group is, a logical approach to decision-making will still be beneficial. However, it must never become a substitute for listening to God. Both are complementary.

Even when God has revealed his will to us, we still need plenty of discussion. God is not likely to give us supernaturally all the details necessary for carrying out his wishes. For example, when my church asked God about his solution to overcrowding, it was clear that we should enlarge the chapel rather than duplicating each service.

We then accepted the responsibility of working out the details, trusting that as we met in Christ's name, the Spirit would guide us. We had to work out the best date for the building work, where the church would meet in the meantime, how much we should spend, and the most appropriate interior design. We didn't await a special revelation for each detail.

I hate muddles. I admit that I tend to overplan and play safe to avoid failure—sometimes I have neglected to ask God what he feels. But muddled thinking rarely glorifies God. Sometimes people label a sloppy approach as Spirit-led! It causes confusion and frustration, leading to strained relationships. Much energy is wasted sorting it all out.

Much of the responsibility for decision-making rests with the chairperson. He or she needs special skills. He may need to learn more about his own role, and then begin the task of educating the rest of the team.

Don't despair if you are not the leader of the team. You can still use your influence to help the group towards better decision-making. This should be done with great subtlety, so that the leader's authority is not usurped. It might be best if he didn't know you were doing it!

May I suggest the following four steps to take:

1. Clear thinking

Before any plan can be drawn up, the issue, problem or goal must be clearly understood. It is too easy to talk in broad generalizations, use abstract words or resort to hairsplitting over minor matters.

Some teams are blessed with one member who helps the group to ask itself the right questions. Two of the groups I belong to have someone of this kind. One is an accountant and the other is a solicitor. Sometimes I think of them as nuisances because they hold up the discussion! But deep down I really value their input.

Sometimes we need a lot more relevant information before we can begin to tackle some issues. It will save time if one of the team is asked to search out more facts. Recently, the college tutors were asked to discuss the problem of work overload among second-year students. 'Most of them can't cope,' we were told. I decided to get some facts. It emerged that only two or three were in serious difficulties. One had been ill. Another was a slow worker. The third had not used his time wisely. End of discussion!

Your team may need to decide that another group would be more appropriate to make a certain decision. A basic rule to follow is that decisions should be made as near as possible to the people doing the work. A problem in the Sunday School should normally be solved by the team of teachers rather than the elders.

Where there are several levels of leadership we must decide which group should make particular decisions. Take youth work for example. The church may have a PCC, a group of elders and a team of youth leaders. Which group is appropriate to work out each particular issue?

The Evangelical Alliance has three levels—the staff team, the Executive Committee and the Board of Management. (I sit on the latter two.) Who should decide about issues like holidays, setting up an event like Leadership '84, employing a part-time secretary or buying a new computer?

At Cranleigh Chapel we have eighteen deacons (sixteen men, and two women who work alongside their husbands). Each deacon is head of a team which is responsible for a specific aspect of church life such as transport, finances, and literature. Rather than being raised at the monthly meeting of all eighteen (which deals only with major matters) most issues are dealt with by each department. We also have a group of seven elders who are responsible for the spiritual life of the church.

2. Developing alternatives

Unless God has revealed only one solution or goal, then it is wise to consider alternatives. It is not a good idea to choose the first thing that comes to mind. To make the right choice we need facts, opinions and ideas. Making decisions without enough facts is dangerous. On the other hand we can be too analytical, so that we never decide anything.

How do you collect information and develop various alternatives? You could involve the whole team. Or you could ask one or two people to put their heads together to prepare a paper for the whole team to discuss. This is a great time saver.

We often do this at Moorlands. Before we launched Moorlands School of Christian Studies (evening classes for local Christians) we asked the Director of Studies, John Hosier, to prepare a paper outlining several alternatives. We each received a copy well in advance of the meeting. The final discussion was relatively brief because John had done his homework well. At present, Tim Marks, Director of Pastoral Studies, is preparing material on in-service training of pastors.

3. Making the decision

Some teams live in cloud-cuckoo land. Their decisions are total non-starters. I'm all for feet-on-the-ground realism. I like to ask awkward questions like 'Can it be done?', 'Are people willing to do it?' and 'Have we the resources?' Boring questions like that!

We must remember that someone must bear the burden of a group decision. When we planned the Moorlands School of Christian Studies, most tutors knew that for a whole term it would mean an extra evening's work each week, plus preparation time.

We need to take a much wider view than just the issue itself. How is it going to affect other people? On one occasion in college we decided to have a time of prayer and fasting over the lunch hour. It was a good decision in itself. What we hadn't considered was that mothers and young children are normally present at lunchtimes. You couldn't ask toddlers to fast! So we arranged for a meal to be prepared for them.

Even a correct decision can fall flat on its face if it is implemented at the wrong time. Sometimes we act in haste, and regret it later. And often we fall into the opposite trap; we procrastinate because we are frightened to go forward.

4. Commitment to action

It is quite easy to decide something and then forget that steps must be taken to actually *do* it. We often assume that someone else is getting on with it. It is the chairman's job to see that the appropriate people are selected to take action.

At our church leaders' meetings we discuss things like applicants for baptism and membership. Since we interview people personally, each meeting results in people who must be contacted.

A recent college staff meeting recommended certain students for particular career opportunities. We recorded their names in the staff minutes. Great! What we didn't do was to commit a staff member to passing on the job descriptions to the students. So nothing was done.

Three things would prevent this kind of mix-up. One is the responsibility of the chairman, the other two that of the minute taker.

First, the chairman should ask one of the team to carry out the decision. Second, the decision should be clearly recorded—'Derek Copley to see Joe Bloggs about the assistant pastorate in Hull.' Third, his initials should be placed in the left hand margin so that a quick glance will reveal that he is supposed to do something. He can then read the paragraph opposite to inform him of his commitment.

Whenever possible I like to see things down in black and white. Sometimes it is valuable to record both the decision and some details of the discussion. It is invaluable to have copies given to each team member. In spite of time pressures they should be handed out as soon as possible. For example, a list of deacons who have agreed to interview potential church members is not much good six weeks after the meeting. Theoretically, team members ought to make their own personal notes during the discussion. In practice, most people tend to rely on their set of minutes for their information.

How does your team do things?

May I suggest that you analyse what is really happening within your own team discussions? Think about that last meeting you had. Observe what happens at your next meeting. You'll learn a lot!

Here are some questions to ask yourself. How are decisions usually made? Does one person dominate? Do two people get their way by loudly supporting each other? Does a minority or majority ignore the feelings of the rest of the group? Is anything preventing you from using the consensus approach? Are some people afraid to let others air their views, and consequently won't allow a true consensus to be reached?

Are you clear about the best steps towards making good decisions? Are you using committees and individuals to serve the team by looking for alternatives and searching out information?

Is there a right balance between a business-like approach and taking time to listen to God?

Why not share these things with your team? See what the others feel—'Hey, listen to what Derek Copley has written about . . . .' Is your team strong enough to make an open discussion possible? It could make a big difference to future meetings.

7

Being Part of a Team

As a leader, who do you consider to be the most important people in your church? Is it those you care for pastorally, like the members of the house group? Or the ladies who attend the women's meeting? Or the Sunday School kids you teach? Should everyone be equally important, so that you attempt to relate on the same level to all of them? What about the others on the leadership team? Where do they fit in? Fellow committee members on the PCC, youth leadership team or senior citizens organizers —how do you decide?

We each have to work out our priorities. In our honest desire to be absolutely fair by spreading our efforts evenly across the church, we may neglect some key relationships which need nurturing more than others.

When you work out your priorities, some people necessarily have to be placed at the bottom of the list. Whom should that include? For me it has to be church members for whom I have no special responsibility or working relationship. I don't mean that we should ignore people or refuse to offer help when there is an obvious need which God wants us to meet. But there are only twenty-four hours in a day and we must make provision for our devotional lives, families, careers and relaxation.

Next on the list are the men, women and children for

whom we are responsible. We would seek to form closer relationships with them than we do with most other church members. Here there is more than just a casual acquaintance. They are especially looking to us for pastoral care, so we should give them a higher proportion of our time.

At the top of the list is your team. Maybe you work alone and don't belong to a team. Or perhaps you call it something different, and don't even recognize that it is a team. I would like to define a team as a group of leaders who work together to achieve something—such as the deacons, elders, or those responsible for the 25–50s or the youth work

If you are the leader of the team, I hope this chapter will help you to do it more effectively. If you are simply a member of a team, then what follows may enable you to make a better contribution and to educate other members. Maybe those readers who have no team at all will consider inviting people to work with them.

As the principal of a Bible College you might expect me to make the students my priority. In fact it's not the students but the staff team—the chef, secretaries, the bursar, estate manager and the tutors. They come first. (I hope students reading this will forgive me!)

I do give plenty of time to the students, probably about twenty hours a week, especially to the eleven in my tutor group. My greatest concern though is for the staff. Without my care for them and the mutual ministry into each other's lives, what they do among the students will not be effective. Also, the observed relationships among us should be an example to the students. The way we treat each other will be a model to follow now and in the future.

Jesus had a team—the twelve disciples. He had priorities too. His Father came first. He withdrew from everyone to be alone with God. The disciples came next. He withdrew from crowds to be with them. Even among the twelve he had special friends with whom he spent more time (Peter, James and John). And it would seem that John came top of the list. Then came the seventy. Finally, there were the multitudes.

Team leader or manager?

There is a world of difference between a leader who is genuinely part of a team and one who sees himself or herself as its boss. The former is biblical, the latter tends to be based on Western secular thinking. It is a living body. (By the way, I firmly believe in Christian management and in positive leadership.)

Let me show you a summary of these two alternatives.[1]

	Team man/woman	Boss
Support	Each member supports the others including the leader. Each gives, each receives.	The leader expects support for himself.
Timing	All the members work together to decide when the time is right.	The people wait for the leader to give the word.
Relationships	There is a high degree of equality between team members. Each regards the others as important.	There is a fixed and clear cut hierarchy and relationships are seen in terms of how each individual relates to the leader.
Dynamism	The team works	The people are fol-

---

[1]Adapted from Christian Leadership letter, June/July 1983. Marc Europe.

	Team man/woman	*Boss*
	things out together. They are inter-dependent.	lowers and look to the leader for the answers. They are dependent on him.
Decision making	Usually by consensus or a system of voting.	Decisions are made at the top and are com-municated 'down'. He knows best what to do. All communication flows through the leader.
Goals	There is a common goal arrived at by the group. They work together to achieve it.	The leader may have developed the goal. Because he feels he 'owns' it he controls it. Its success largely depends on his drive and vision.

I'm not suggesting that every attitude and action listed on the right is evil. Clearly it isn't. However, you may find the summary useful in assessing whether you have the kind of approach suitable for developing a team. The way you view others on the team, and their relationships to you, will determine how effective the team will be.

In an earlier chapter I criticized weak leadership. Now it appears that I'm against strong leadership too! Let me assure you I'm not. People today are looking for leadership that knows where it's going, men and women who are prepared to take a definite lead, especially in a time of crisis. They want to be served by those to whom God reveals his heart, but who nevertheless share what they arc hearing with each other and the church.

I have always been a team person. To my shame I have often failed, because I'm something of a coward. Even when it was perfectly right and proper to make decisions on my own, I haven't always done it. I have feared unpopularity. I have put the matter on the agenda for a team discussion, so that I could use the leadership group as a wall behind which to hide. 'This isn't really my decision. I'm only carrying out the wishes of the committee. Don't blame me, blame the team.' Perhaps you have done the same.

When is a team not a team?

There is quite a lot of self-deception when it comes to teams. Some people believe they are part of a team but aren't, because it's not really a team at all. Power-seekers often refer to *my* team—my deacons, staff etc. (with the emphasis on *my*). What they mean is that they are in charge of a group of people who do as they're told. That's not a team.

Nor is a team a gathering of individuals who come together to fight things out, each striving to get the others to see it his way, refusing to examine alternatives. It is not just a series of neat little organizational boxes with names written in them. Some teams are really only committees, because they merely meet to make decisions and then each goes off to do his own thing—there is no real working together.

Having said that, let me correct any impression that a team is a group of think-alikes who talk sweetly over cups of tea. The best teams are a real mixture of outlooks and temperaments with healthy tensions. Yes, I believe in tensions—provided the team is mature enough to make them productive.

A motor car has an accelerator, a brake pedal and a

gear stick. A team is the same. The accelerator is the visionary who is ready to reach ninety miles per hour in 6.2 seconds, leaving a cloud of dust behind him. On his own he would be dangerous—his pace and innovations would split the church. He needs people who are brakes, to slow him down. Yet without the accelerator, the brakes would prevent real progress. The gear-changers are the wise men and women who can discern just when the church or group should move into higher gear, or drop down again because the venture has proved too risky.

The use of teams is not only practical but biblical. The New Testament assumes that leaders will work in groups. This pattern of working is not only more effective but acts as a visual aid in teaching others. Relationships between team members will be noticed by church members. This will influence them in their own relationships because people are imitators. (Hopefully they will see a good example rather than a poor one!) When I led a team of teachers doing seminars at Spring Harvest, one of my aims was that we should work together in such a way that the delegates would benefit from what they had observed.

I belong to several teams including the eldership of my church, the BMMF personnel committee, the Evangelical Alliance executive committee and the Moorlands staff. The college team is the one in which I am most deeply involved. What a mixture it is! Definitely not a bunch of Yes-men and Yes-women. They are as varied as the disciples. There's ex-missionary John Davis, with his passionate concern for the third world, who enjoys provoking students. I'm the one with his feet rather too firmly on the ground (probably because I'm a former scientist). Robin Wood, the college bursar, appears to have only one aim in life—to grab as much money as he can (well, that's what we pretend!). Stuart, an evangelist, charms us all with his flamboyant ties; and estate manager David Hortop scares us all with his hair-raising tales of life in the Brazilian jungle.

What about the idea of a leader among leaders? Is there never a case for someone being *the* leader? Must this be avoided at all costs? Certainly not! For example Timothy, in New Testament times, held a prominent position. What really matters is a person's motivation. Attitude is more important than position. I deplore the man or woman who sets out deliberately to seize leadership by riding roughshod over others. The healthiest situation is often when someone simply emerges as a leader, without having sought the position. Authority is thrust on him. Rather than boasting about his own rank, he will be proud of his team and will seek help and advice from his colleagues. His most striking attribute will not be his power but the fact that he cares for the church more than anyone else on the team. He will carry the largest burden.

If you haven't a team how do you create one?

Some leaders feel threatened by genuine team work. They see themselves as bosses who issue instructions to their fellow committee members. This may be the result of insecurity and fear. Fear of sharing power. Fear that someone with more gifts may emerge. Fear that if others do too much, they'll make a mess of things. Or it may be that they are unable to form close working relationships —he or she is happier functioning alone. At times the cut and thrust of group discussion results in people's ideas being attacked or rejected. Some leaders interpret this as personal rejection, and avoid team work altogether.

On the other hand there are leaders who would love to have a team but have to work alone. How do you create one, especially where there may be no machinery available for doing it officially? The fact that a team may not be recognized doesn't invalidate it. It can still be a team.

What kind of people should you invite to join you?

Above all, you need diversity. If most of the team were avid prophets you would probably lurch from one vision to another. If they were all evangelists you would get worn out with endless ventures. Diversity, yes, but they need to be compatible too, both with you and each other. And may I suggest that you don't invite people who are likely to be pains in the neck!

What is the purpose of a team?

Some people are 'into' teams. (Like others are 'into' healing or deliverance ministry.) But do they know why? Are they actually functioning as teams or are they just following a trend? This raises the basic question: 'What is a team meant to do and how should it go about it?'

A team should be two things if it is to be effective. First, it is to be productive—making plans which will enhance prayer, worship, personal growth and evangelism. Second, a team must take steps to nourish itself spiritually. Only then will it really be capable of leading the house group or Sunday School. A congregation builds itself up in love when the members serve one another using their spiritual gifts (Eph 4:16). On a smaller scale, team members are to do the same within the group.

Unfortunately, many teams tend to emphasize one at the expense of the other. They should be doing *both*. Those who focus mainly on tasks eventually become less productive. They become nothing more than committees with heavy agendas, a brief opening prayer and meetings that often go on late into the night. There is little time to concentrate on the team members themselves—their hurts, feelings, aspirations, and ambitions. Such a group is like a machine.

Groups which place too high a priority on personal growth are usually very happy. They are like a kind of country club with its pleasant congenial atmosphere. Very cosy! However, they produce very little. They go home from their meetings with warm feelings towards each other and the church, but they will have done very little serious planning and decision-making. It is the church which suffers, because it doesn't get the leadership it deserves.

Three years ago I discovered the need for balance. It came as a bombshell. I realized that several leadership groups to which I belonged had neglected to build each other up. I decided to try and do something about it at our next joint elders/deacons meeting. What worried me was that we only had a total of two hours available. Would we get through the agenda if I allocated half an hour to a time of fellowship? I decided to risk it.

I began with a short Bible reading and some brief comments. Then I invited people to share things for prayer (not church matters but personal things). In the remaining fifteen minutes we prayed for each other. It worked! The discussion and decision-making was done in a warm atmosphere. Instead of 'losing' half an hour and finishing late, we completed the business early. We discovered that if you put relationships first, then the tasks are accomplished more effectively.[1]

Making sure the team grows

Before we are likely to do anything constructive, we need to be convinced that building up the team is not just an optional extra. To do it needs courage and self-discipline. Courage, because we see non-productive time as 'wasted' time. Self-discipline, because we may forget after a while that the team needs nourishing, and our meetings become nothing more than business discussions.

---

[1] I have written more fully on the subject in chapter 10 of *My Chains Fell Off* (Paternoster, 1982).

I was recently invited to meet with a group of dejected church deacons. They were in a state of disarray, and so was the church. The congregation was looking to them for guidance, yet they weren't providing any. Why? Because their own relationships were shallow, tense and mistrusting. As a group they couldn't hear what God was saying. The team was divided. Their decisions were hesitant and the church knew it.

A team will only exercise good leadership when there is love and trust. Relationships need to be established in which members feel free to allow their weaknesses to be known to the others, without fear of rejection. They can relax because there is no need to put on a front.

They will have a pride in each other both in private and in public. They will hear one another and they will hear God's voice.

Some people feel obliged to limit their closest friendships to other members of the team. There is no obligation to do this. We should not feel guilty if the people who support us are not fellow elders or youth leaders.

How do you create a team of this kind? With difficulty! It takes hard work and sometimes involves pain. There is often the temptation to revert back to becoming a committee.

There are many ways to do it but they all have one thing in common—they involve getting to know one another. Food may be the answer! That is, getting together in pairs or as a group to share a meal. Sometimes the urgent must be left to take care of itself. Practically everything was urgent in Jesus' life, yet he frequently withdrew from the crowds who needed him in order to sustain his relationship with the Twelve.

We need to be willing to receive as well as give out. Some of us find this very difficult. I am especially reluctant voluntarily to let others know my needs. Recently, while my wife was in hospital a colleague asked if he could relieve me of one of my Sunday Services. I graciously declined. I thought about it later and realized how pig-headed I had been. I really did need the help. I then went along to his study and admitted my stubbornness and accepted his genuine offer.

Some teams celebrate the Lord's Supper or have times of praise and testimony. We did that at our half-day retreat for the Moorlands staff. We talked, prayed, met round the Lord's table and finally we had lunch together in a private room in a local restaurant. We have also planned a Christmas meal together in Dorchester (no, not *at* the Dorchester!) and a house-warming party for new staff member Tim and his wife Olga.

There is nothing to stop us building each other up while we discuss business matters. How? By encouraging and praising each other's contributions to the discussion. By finding ways of reconciling differences and disagreements which might lead to tensions. By giving in when the issue is not a vital one. By admitting we're wrong, or saying 'sorry'.

'That's all very cosy and nice, but you obviously haven't got the kind of team I have to put up with,' you might say. Yes, I appreciate that most of us belong to teams we didn't select. Incidentally—I wonder if the Twelve felt that way about each other? I can't think that big-mouth Peter and pessimistic Thomas were always considered to be assets by the others.

My advice is 'Don't complain, do something!' Accept those whom you've got and give yourself to them. You may be pleasantly surprised at what happens when you focus on building one another up. People change and relationships develop as you learn to grow together. As a last resort you might want to pray for God's reselection of the team!

8

Motivating Others

The majority of those who earn a salary or wages have to sign a contract of employment. Sometimes there is also a job description. Because they are paid for their work they have little choice but to do what is required of them. Most of us have a boss of some kind, and there is an obligation to do as he requests. Failure to do those things could result in a telling-off, punishment or even dismissal. On the whole we tend to accept this system as reasonably fair—you are paid to work, so you must simply get on with it. We are motivated to do what someone else expects because there is a financial reward, even if we don't necessarily like what we do.

Churches are different. Most people are volunteers. With the exception of paid staff like the pastor, no one is under any obligation whatsoever to do any of the tasks they are asked to do (or even attend church). They are free to walk out whenever they please. If they don't want to teach a Sunday School class or attend their local house group, they don't have to. If they are bored by evening services they can stay at home and goggle at the telly.

At times those of us who are leaders have to cope with our own lack of motivation. We also have to try to encourage others to serve God effectively under our guidance, even if there are only half a dozen in our care.

Some people are what I call 'self-starters'—they are highly motivated and little effort is needed to persuade them to work for God. Others are quite the opposite— even putting a bomb under them wouldn't shift them!

Churches are not like secular organizations with an end product and profits. So what is it that we are trying to motivate people towards? I would suggest two things —first 'being', and second 'doing'.

Primarily we are in the position of leadership to help people grow towards personal Christ-likeness of character. This needs a high level of motivation to achieve success. The required development will only come about through hard work and perseverance. It is our privilege to help them to take the steps which will bring about that change of character—such as establishing richer devotional lives, and learning through the joys and sorrows of personal relationships.

Our second aim is Christian service. According to the New Testament, every Christian is meant to be active. Ephesians 4 says that it is the task of leaders to *train*. It isn't enough to teach people what they ought to be doing. Unless they are motivated to work for God, then we have not achieved our aims. Ideally, each person in our house group or women's fellowship should be using his or her spiritual gifts both inside the group and outside. Some Christians will be called by God to serve full-time overseas, but will their motivation be high enough actually to get up and go?

To take another example: tithing is biblical. If every believer gave a tenth or more of his income there would be massive resources available for extending the kingdom worldwide. Sadly, few give very much more than a quarter of that amount. How can we persuade them? Again, at the most elementary level of commitment, we want people to attend the services and other meetings appropriate to them. The fact that in some churches only

20% of the membership attends the mid-week prayer meeting means that for various reasons the absent majority is not motivated enough to be there.

As leaders, God gives us the ability to discern what is good for people. But we are not managers of an organization, so we can't simply issue instructions to them. So how do we convince them to take action? Do we spend more time explaining things personally, pray more for them, preach better sermons, give them more praise, or what? Do we follow Nehemiah's example, who tried to encourage his followers to do what he knew was right? Tobiah had moved into a room which wasn't his, so Nehemiah grabbed all his household effects and chucked them out (Neh 13:7–9). A group of tradesmen were hanging about outside the city wall at night time on the Sabbath, so Nehemiah threatened to 'lay hands' on them (and not in the New Testament sense, either!). His tactics were effective—'From that time on they no longer came on the Sabbath' (v.21). And he attempted to dissuade the men from marrying the wrong women by beating them and pulling out their hair (v.25)!

Are these strong-arm methods right for the church today—or is there a better way? Before making a decision, we really ought to understand more about the nature of motivation itself.

What is motivation?

Lawrence Crabb defines motivation as 'the energy or force which results in specific behaviour'.[1] His term 'specific behaviour' is what I have already called 'the change to Christ-likeness and Christian service'—these being the two aims of leadership. How can we provide the right

---

[1]Lawrence J. Crabb Jr, *Effective Biblical Counselling* (Zondervan), p.76.

conditions so that enough of that motivational energy is released to enable people to pursue their God-given goals?

Most worthwhile aspects of personal growth and Christian work involve considerable self-sacrifice—that is, putting others first and ourselves second. For a normal human being this is an unnatural way in which to behave, so the motivational drive is low. Man (even Christian man) is basically self-centred. Our self-centredness drives us to try to meet our own personal needs rather than fulfil those of others (which is what Christian service is all about). We are highly motivated to receive support and words of encouragement, but when it comes to encouraging others, we seem to have little drive in that direction. Because the pressure created by emotional needs is so strong, even the nicest people can manipulate their friends to satisfy themselves. There is no shortage of energy driving us to take from others. And if a presently met need is threatened, a mighty power arises from within to protect it.

What exactly are those needs we are talking about? Crabb summarizes them in two words—significance and security. I prefer a somewhat more detailed list—love, belonging, acceptance, purpose and significance. We also have physical appetites like eating, drinking and sleeping, as well as spiritual needs.

In theory Christians shouldn't need to seek satisfaction continually from other people (self-centredness) but should receive help and fulfilment direct from God. If this were to become a practical reality in our lives, our predominant driving force would be towards God's goals for us—growth and service.[1]

Every day of our lives, and probably dozens of times a

---

[1] I have written more fully about this in chapters 9–13 of my book *Ears to Hear* (Kingsway Publications 1984).

day, our various emotional needs make us feel uncomfortable. Subconsciously we set ourselves goals which we believe will satisfy those needs. We take steps whereby we hope we will achieve them. The need is therefore satisfied, just as thirst is quenched after a drink of water. What is happening is that we are involved in a cycle (or vicious circle) which commences each time with a felt need and ends in fulfilment. Some writers call it a 'deficit cycle' and express the uncomfortable thought that most people are trapped by such cycles and therefore remain self-centred and unproductive in their Christian lives. This explains to some degree why the inner drive in the right direction is often so low.

Abraham Maslow, a psychologist who has carefully researched the field of motivation, has some helpful things to say in this area. Without being too technical it is worth while summarizing what he has found.

As leaders we often complain that those we lead are not motivated to do what is right. If I understand Maslow correctly, there is sometimes a simple explanation for this.

There is a motivational driving force inside everyone, and it causes people to behave in a particular way. As Crabb says: 'All behaviour is motivated.' When we complain that people lack motivation, we are really saying that they don't want to do the particular thing we feel they should do (such as door-to-door visitation). Their driving force is in another direction, because an unmet need is crying out for attention. For example, the person who lacks interest in talking about Christ may feel a strong sense of rejection. He will take steps to meet his need for acceptance because it is creating far more pressure than his desire for evangelism.

Maslow divides human needs into five categories: physiological needs (food, water, sleep), the need for safety, the need for belonging, the need for esteem, and the need for self-actualization (personal growth and service). He lists them in the form of a hierarchy:

> self-actualization
> purpose
> love
> security
> physical

As we can see, growth and service come top of the list —they are the highest things we can attain. For the Christian, they represent all that God wants us to be and do.

Unfortunately, the needs lower down in the hierarchy create the strongest pressures, and the higher ones the weakest. Maslow says that until the greater deficits of the more basic needs are met, people will not be motivated to achieve the higher things. They are trapped in the deficit cycle. People in the West are not trapped by the lowest ones, physiological and safety, but by the emotional needs like belonging and esteem (which I have labelled love, belonging, acceptance, purpose and significance).

If Maslow is right, then some Christians will only have a concern for service and personal development when their lower needs are satisfied more fully. If they aren't, then the weaker drive to work for God will be swamped by the force urging them to meet their emotional deficits. There was a classic case of this in the time of the Exodus. God had promised the people deliverance from their suffering, but, 'They did not listen to him because of their discouragement and cruel bondage' (Ex 6:9). The nobler call, to hear the voice of God, went unheeded because a lower need was unfulfilled due to their terrible suffering.

The implications of this are enormous. As leaders we want people to develop the seven-fold fruit of the Spirit described in Galatians 5, and we want them to use their spiritual gifts for the enrichment of others. Try as we might, some people simply won't respond. Why? There are probably several reasons, but one of them may be that they are preoccupied with the pressures created by their lower needs. They are so concerned to search for sources of fulfilment that they have little energy left for spiritual pursuits.

Realistically, we must accept that some people will never attempt great things for God, no matter what we may do. Others might, if we can provide loving and patient pastoral care to meet those powerful lower needs. They need to be released from their deficit cycles to work on a higher plane of pleasing God. More and more Christians are struggling today with emotional wounds as the quality of family life decreases. To issue them with spiritual commands may sound very commendable, but it ignores the very real barriers to those commands ever being obeyed.

What gets up their noses?
(Or: what are we doing that demotivates people?)

To be realistic, even if we were virtually perfect in our leadership, it wouldn't guarantee that others would be motivated. Often some factors are beyond our control—domestic crises, sudden illness, redundancy. But we can be sure that we will demotivate people if our leadership is generally poor or of the wrong kind.

Bad administration causes frustration, anger and apathy. If the decisions about what course of action to take are not clearly thought through, or are communicated badly, we generate confusion. Or if changes are made without people being consulted first, they are likely to be angry and unco-operative. Sometimes people haven't a clue why they are doing a certain thing, and they eventually lose interest because there are no definite goals to work for. Maybe they are not trained or shown how to do the work, and feel a sense of failure. Before long they will give up.

Neutral or poor relationships among colleagues may discourage some people. If too much emphasis is placed on achievement and too little on team relationships, there will not be enough mutual support, which is so valuable in times of struggle. Maybe there is jealousy because one or two are not pulling their weight, or are given more rewarding and interesting jobs to do.

Perhaps the greatest demotivator of all is the feeling that no one cares about you—especially if that impression comes from the leader. Last May, after three tiring weeks at Spring Harvest, I came back to college to find negative attitudes among quite a number of students. When I enquired what was wrong, several confessed that because one tutor was moving house, three were at Spring Harvest and one had simply disappeared that week, they felt helpless and abandoned—nobody really cared about them—there was no one to go to.

Even the most highly motivated person will eventually reduce his efforts if he feels that no one cares. Why bother, if no one notices you or acknowledges what you are doing? People aren't always seeking status, but they do need encouragement. Lack of praise or personal concern makes them feel that their work is not all that important anyway. This is especially true if a leader doesn't really listen when people complain—they feel rejected.

This week I was telephoned by a very upset Christian executive. He used to be a highly motivated person, always at his desk and ready to do his utmost to please his superior. But the leader above him never seemed to have the time to stop and listen. He simply issued instructions every so often. Slowly, the man's enthusiasm declined and only reluctantly did he do as he was asked. He had become discouraged and demotivated.

What turns them on?

Suppose you removed all the negative factors described above, would that be enough? No! People need more than just the absence of things that discourage them. They thrive best when there are things to encourage them to move forward.

They respond best to leaders who know where they're going. I don't mean the well-dressed, smoothy-type TV salesman. I am talking about men and women who are clearly in touch with God. They are not dictatorial, yet they give a definite lead. They are people of integrity— you can trust them to be reliable, to keep promises and confidences and to be consistent both in public and in private.

Recognition and praise are not essential but they are helpful and much appreciated. We can easily do small things like thanking individuals publicly for the contribution they have made to church life or evangelism. Or we can ask for their names to be mentioned in the church magazine when appropriate.

People are at their most motivated when they are doing what they really want to do. So one of the best ways of helping people to be in that happy position is to ask them to be involved in planning. People are much more committed to something in which they have had a say. It also makes them feel part of the church, not mere employees working for an institution.

Working towards a definite goal is attractive, especially if the plan or project has been jointly arrived at. It gives a sense of achievement—once you know where you're going, you'll know when you have arrived! As one writer put it: 'Goals are great motivators.' By goals, I don't mean humanly devised bright ideas, but faith-aims arrived at through prayer and discussion.

After a while some people need a fresh challenge. They grow stale after doing the same thing for years. Often they are ready for greater responsibility.

Getting your own way by manipulation

Have you ever had the awful feeling, when it's too late, that you've agreed to something which you really had no intention of doing? You feel cheated; conned and resentful because someone has succeeded in getting you to fulfil his wishes against your own better judgement. This is totally different from normal methods of persuasion which leave you free to say yes or no. I am talking about methods which are underhand because they put you on the spot with no real freedom of choice. It's called manipulation.

But do you ever do it yourself? Do I? Until recently I was sure I had never used such means to get my way. I had to change my mind after reading *Keys to Effective Motivation* by R.M. McDonough (Broadman). Time and time again I saw myself portrayed and it gave me quite a jolt. I feel it is worth while exposing some of the wrong methods we may be using—often without meaning to.

As leaders we have a God-given responsibility to influence other people, both for their own enrichment and for the benefit of the church. It isn't wrong to want them to move in a certain direction and to try to steer them that way. But are we urging them to do things which are genuinely for their own good, to do the things that happen to suit us? And how are we persuading them—by fair means or foul?

Manipulators aren't always aggressive dictators who exert irresistible pressure on people until they give in. They can use weakness as a powerful weapon. I call it the 'poor me' technique. Dare one use the word 'blackmail' in a book such as this? In a way, yes. However much we dress it up, that's what some leaders are doing. It's usually emotional blackmail. 'If you don't like the way I record the minutes of this committee, I'll resign,' is typical.

In the final part of this chapter we will examine the proper means to persuade people. Here we will look at some of the undesirable methods. This isn't to say that they are ineffective; unfortunately, they are often *more* effective.

The use of power and aggression can be fairly straight forward. It may come in the form of a threat of dismissal to a deacon or youth leader. Or it may simply be a command put so strongly that the victim dare not disobey. Mutual back-scratching is another misuse of power— 'I'll do this for you if you'll do that for me.'

People have a strong dislike for being put down either privately or publicly. Their fear provides the ideal opening for manipulation. It's quite easy for a leader to get his own way by suggesting that the person is either stupid because he is unwilling, or that he hasn't yet reached sufficient maturity to fully understand the situation. So to avoid feeling stupid, and to appear mature, he gives in. You can force some people into obedience by shaming them in front of their friends.

The 'poor me' approach is used more often than we think. We might persuade those who do not want to obey our commands, by appealing to their more sensitive feelings. We might say: 'You really wouldn't want to hurt me would you?' Or we might try to make people change their minds out of guilt, by behaving like a martyr or using the pathetic 'No one ever listens to me.'

Spiritual blackmail is a very sad abuse of authority. While it is true that leaders should be able to understand God's heart more than most people, they should never misuse their position of respect. It is very tempting when people really trust us implicitly, to claim that God has revealed to us that which *we* want done. You can't argue with God!

Getting them going

It has been said that it is impossible for one person to
motivate another, because it must come from within.
Even so, there is still plenty we can do. Although they
have the ultimate choice, we can influence people's attitudes and actions. We can help to build a climate in
which they may become motivated.

People thrive best when there is an environment of
emotional safety—one involving orderliness, a high
degree of predictability and stability. They feel secure
because they know what's happening. They are not constantly rocked by crises and chaos. Surprisingly, you can
have calmness and at the same time be progressive and
dynamic. They are not mutually exclusive. You can have
both. A poor atmosphere causes people to fight, withdraw
through fear, or simply become apathetic.

The year before last, for a short period of time, we
caused a feeling of insecurity among our third-year students. We had given them both a syllabus and a timetable,
but these were constantly being changed, often without
warning. Occasionally the students would arrive for a
lecture, only to find that it was cancelled because the
tutor was away for the day. It demotivated them, because
there was an air of uncertainty. It led to some anger and
apathy.

You can't be the ideal leader for every person at once.
There will always be an inner struggle to decide which
approach will motivate the maximum number of people.
The way we regard their motivation will determine how
we go about things.

Some leaders believe that most people dislike work,
have little ambition or imagination, and don't want responsibility. As a result they lead in a way that fits in
with their pessimistic beliefs. This type of leader argues
that since people are lazy and unco-operative the only

thing they'll respond to is the stern voice of the autocrat —you tell them what you want done and bully them into accepting your ideas. You would certainly never let them share in decision making or consultation. Only the top people should do the planning! Most of the communication is one way—from you *down* to them, perhaps through a chain of command.

On the other hand, suppose you believe that most people do have imagination and drive. Your optimism will lead to a very different way of inspiring them. Instead of dishing out orders, you will try to create an atmosphere in which their good qualities will emerge, and where they will voluntarily seek responsibility. Instead of telling them what *you* want done there will be discussions and joint decisions. We will assume that this is the appropriate approach for most of those we lead.

Character development

Moorlands Bible College is more than an academic institution. Our aim is to fulfil the higher purposes of growth and service as well as imparting knowledge. We do all kinds of things to motivate students in these areas and we regularly assess their progress. There are classroom teaching, devotional services, group prayer times, and at least twice a term students sit down with their personal tutor to talk things through. We provide both regular and one-off opportunities to work in local churches and even allocate a specific time in the morning for personal devotions.

Does all this guarantee success? The answer is 'no'. You may set aside a thirty-minute time to pray but you cannot force someone to use it profitably. He may talk for an hour with a tutor but it doesn't ensure that he will be motivated to change. It is the same in a church situation. There are several things which leaders may do to provide the right atmosphere for growth. Some will respond, others will not.

Good teaching from the pulpit, in the house group and in face-to-face pastoral situations gives people information, stimulation and challenge. Some guest speakers are particularly effective in motivating people to improve their devotional lives. Reading suitable books like *Celebration of Discipline* by Richard Foster, or attending gatherings on Saturday nights in which there is a stimulating and worshipful atmosphere, all help. The big events like Spring Harvest, Royal Week, Filey, Dales and Downs Weeks should be recommended by us because of the thousands of people who are newly motivated as a result.

Are those we lead really aware of where they should be going spiritually and emotionally? And do they know how to get there, and how to know they are making progress? Do they know that one of our purposes as leaders is to help them, and do we discuss it together when we visit them pastorally? Is it obvious by my life and attitude that I'm making progress so that what they see attracts them, and they want to follow that route themselves?

The most neglected area of all among Christians is their daily quiet time. We struggle with it too. We must do more than make them feel guilty about their failures. It is more constructive to find practical ways to help them re-establish things. Sometimes I invite people to be accountable to me for a while as an incentive to pray and meditate on the Bible.

Planning the work

Many of the initiatives in Christian service will come from us, the leaders. We know that people need to have a purpose to work for, which gives them a sense of achievement afterwards. They will be very much more motivated by an idea which challenges them. Some people don't naturally have a lot of vision and it is our job to give them some. However, we must not cheat people into making something sound better than it really is, because they'll soon go sour and mistrust us. We need to be as realistic as possible, yet remember not to discourage them by over-emphasizing the difficulties.

We can't discuss every detail with everyone. Sometimes we have to delegate. If we do, then we need to use sound management principles to avoid confusion and hurt. Delegation tells someone that you believe in him and trust him to get on with something.

There is nothing more helpful to motivation than being involved in creating ideas and jointly sharing in decisions. People feel much more committed to a work if it's 'ours' rather than merely hatched up by a leader. To ask someone to share is to say: 'I need you. I appreciate you. I want to hear your ideas.' People will often follow our goals gladly, but it is even better if we are able to follow a course of action which was initiated by them.

What about training? Fear of failure stops some people from becoming active. It's not surprising that we meet resistance to serving God—we simply haven't shown them what to do. What gifts do they have? How can those gifts be developed? It isn't necessary for most people to go to Bible College, yet we often assume that is the only place where people can be trained. That is a pity, because most equipping ought to be done at local church level. We may do it ourselves, by gently nudging people in directions relevant to the gift we may think is there. Or we may send them to a conference or invite someone to do a training session in church. At our church we have done both with our Sunday School teachers.

Caring for people as they work

The knowledge that someone cares is a great motivator.

As leaders we will be nothing more than efficient bosses, unless we love those we lead. They must matter more to us than policies and procedures. Often we must sacrifice our own feelings. If people have any suspicion that we are using them to meet our own needs, their willingness to follow will decline rapidly.

The most destructive leadership attitude is one of in-difference. The second worst is criticism. People build up self-esteem through being given significance from others, especially us. If we ignore them or criticize them continually, we will crush that inner driving force. The most constructive thing we can do for people is to 'affirm' them—that is, to help them feel good about themselves and their achievements.

We must never despise or take for granted those who are volunteers. They are worthy of our respect. We must keep the promises we make. We must care how they feel. It is easy to assume that they are prepared to put up with virtually any kind of inconvenience—but they won't. And why should they?

We may not like the fact that some people won't achieve much until we sort out their lower needs. Doing so is both time-consuming and demanding. We'd rather get them moving without 'wasting' time on their emotional deficits. However, it is a fact that people will follow a leader who satisfies their needs and who is generous in praise and appreciation.

Whatever jobs they are doing, large or small, visible or behind the scenes, those whom we lead need to know what they are doing really matters—because it does! We should ask them frequently how they are getting on and let them know that we are actually hearing them. We need to make replies like: 'I hadn't thought of that idea.' Those who are given the opportunity to report back on what they are doing will continue even more enthusiasti-cally because they know that somebody is interested. If no one ever enquires about your work, you wonder if it really needs doing at all.

Ninety-nine per cent of today's church members are volunteers. We cannot leave most of the work to the remaining 1%. It is God's will that the work should be shared. He expects us to lead in such a way that people are given the most favourable conditions under which they may choose to follow.

9

Change Is Here to Stay!

'There is nothing permanent except change,' wrote Heraclitus. It is as true today as it was when he said it hundreds of years ago. And it will go on being true. Change is here to stay. If that prophet of doom Alvin Toffler is correct, and I believe he is, change will get faster and faster, like a runaway train.

Think of the changes over the past few years. Computer technology has crept into many areas of everyday life—from electronic toys and motor cars to banking and building design. In our supermarket some products have disappeared but we can now buy a whole new range of foods which previously could only have been purchased abroad. Communications systems have changed out of all recognition. Last Autumn I was able to dial direct from India to a rural village in Dorset. We have even more TV channels to choose from as well as the advantages of seeing pictures of what is happening in almost any part of the world within hours of an event. Medical and agricultural methods have changed apace, as have clothing styles. Attitudes and standards within society seem to change almost annually.

Many of the so called 'advances' sometimes make life more difficult than before. Modern equipment and fancy gadgets often cannot be repaired because some shops don't carry spares or prefer to sell you a new one. Many things can't be done without filling in complicated forms or following confusing procedures. The increasing use of electronics has made us seem less important as persons; we end up obeying the machines which are supposed to be our servants. We may eat better food, yet our countryside and rivers are being polluted by pesticides and fertilizers as a result. The wide variety of TV programmes provide more viewing opportunities than ever before, yet it has opened the door to unhelpful or harmful material being beamed into our homes and lives. Many changes in society are for the worse, with a continued increase in burglaries, violent crime and divorce.

Although we complain about the changes we don't like, many things are better than they were. We can buy goods more cheaply and easily at discount stores, using computer technology. More and more bills can be paid conveniently and automatically by the bank without our having to write out cheques or post letters. The existence of supermarkets and hypermarkets makes shopping so much more convenient as the pace of life accelerates. The increasing number of fast take-away (or eat-in) food services also help to conserve our valuable time. New drugs and medical advances have taken away the fear of many illnesses and diseases. Today there is a new awareness of minority groups such as the blacks, the claustrophobics, and the mentally and physically handicapped—an awareness which is creating better attitudes in society.

We have to learn to adapt to all these changes. Surprisingly this includes the so called 'good' ones too—like moving to a nicer home, getting engaged, or buying a new car. Our emotions have to adjust to these things just as much as to the things we find unpleasant, and this causes us to suffer stress. It is for this reason that missionary societies sometimes delay sending couples overseas until they have been married a year. It isn't that they are unsuited to each other, or that living overseas will be intolerable—it's just that people can only adapt slowly to change, and too many new things all at once can cause problems.

Certain people are more adventurous than others and thrive on change. For them, the invention of the self-service petrol pump was a sheer delight. To others it was a nightmare, producing fear and terror. It was reported that one poor confused man had even tried to stuff pound notes up the nozzle. When Britain adopted decimal currency, a shopkeeper in the West Country refused to abandon pounds, shillings and pence because he felt sure that the new coinage wouldn't catch on in his part of the world.

One couple may go to the same holiday resort each year, but their neighbours travel to different places. A man may stick with one hobby all his life, whereas his workmate may try all kinds of new ones. I don't particularly like having new clothes, but an evangelist I know seems to have a new suit on every time I see him.

No two people react to change in exactly the same way. Those who struggle may wonder how some of their friends cope so easily. And the people who simply love adventure wish they could shake some life into people whose lives they consider to be dull and monotonous.

We are all schizophrenic where change is concerned

It's understandable that people should be different from each other, yet as individuals we seem to be quite inconsistent in our handling of new situations. We appear to be two people at the same time. At one moment we have a strong sense of adventure and long to break free. The next day we cling fiercely to what is familiar and safe. Within us there is a constant conflict between the natural instinct to try new and exciting things, and something

like the law of gravity which tries to force us to seek
security in what we know and trust. We fear letting go in
case we lose something valuable and become impover-
ished. Sometimes, what began as a great new venture
loses its value; yet we are unwilling to give it up. And
there are people who hop from one idea to another,
never content to settle down to anything.

Puzzling though it is, we have both the need to hold on
to what we have, and at the same time the urge to be free
to try something else. Our reactions to possible changes
can be as variable as the weather. If the circumstances
and timing are right, then we'll agree; if not, we may dig
our heels in.

It's the job of leaders to help the churches to change

What kind of people make up a Christian congregation?
Just normal men and women like the ones we've described. In daily life we are all bombarded by pressure and
change outside our control. Our slender resources are
constantly drained as we try to adapt to each new situation.
No wonder it's so difficult for churches to move forward.

In the last five to ten years, some congregations have
experienced several major changes in rapid succession.
More established church members are left wondering what
will happen next. I can remember in my own church
when some of the teenage girls stopped wearing head-
coverings. Then some of us began praying in modern
English and used RSV Bibles instead of King James.
Soon women were invited to pray audibly in the prayer
meeting, and later, in the main worship service. Even
though these changes occurred over several years, they
produced deep fears and anxieties in some people. It had
happened too rapidly for them and they couldn't adapt
quickly enough.

Sometimes leaders are tempted to ride roughshod over

people in order to make progress. If the church were merely a secular organization maybe that is what would happen. The powers that be could decide to implement certain ideas regardless of what the workforce felt. They would be left with only two choices—either to go along with it or look for another job.

But a church is not an organization, and we are not its managers. It is a living body, composed not of a salaried workforce but volunteers who are our brothers and sisters. As leaders we are their servants, not their masters. We have no right to try to force results or impose our wills on theirs. All we can do is to seek to establish loving relationships and try to create the kind of atmosphere where people will grow and desire the changes which God wants.

Because we are not to demand allegiance from people, it does not mean that we can abdicate all responsibility. The churches are looking to us to provide competent leadership. While some of us may suffer from a power complex, for others quite the opposite is true—we are reluctant to lead. It is often easier to sit back and let things happen. That way, you don't get into trouble!

Being a person who tries to make things happen is a risky business. Failure lurks around each corner. Success can be dangerous too, because it often leads to further consequences which we hadn't bargained for.

It's not easy to be the right kind of leader at the right time. In the past I have gone from one extreme to the other. Sometimes I have tended to let things take their own course for the sake of peace. At other times I have tried to initiate something new without thinking carefully enough about it. I remember introducing a 'Scripture Song' in my church for the first time, soon after such things had been discovered. I really got into hot water!

Some books describe leaders who try to make things happen as 'change agents'. To me, the term sounds rather too business like and aggressive. It's true that some people do want leaders who are progressive, but they want them to be the kind of people who take the trouble to step into their shoes before they try to do anything. They want us to recognize their fears and misgivings and to bear them in mind. To do that we must know where people are 'at' in their attitude and thinking, as well as where we see the church going. They are looking to us for a wise and clear perception of how God's plan may be carried out. They need the assurance that their own ideas and talents will be put to good use. It is our responsibility to know how the church may arrive at the right decisions, and what is the best timing. We need to be realistic about resistance to change and whether to skirt round it, meet it head on, or abandon that particular idea altogether.

Some congregations need modernization, others need transformation

Today there are more changes taking place in the churches than we are probably aware of. And they are happening faster than ever before. Years ago, the drab brown walls and beige linoleum might have lasted thirty years. Because people moved house less often, and most churches were not growing, there was great stability in the congregation. In doctrine and practice things tended to continue more or less as they were. Often, pastors would spend most of their working life in the same church. It is not so today.

Some aspects of church life need only a little modernization, although in some cases the word transformation might better describe what would be best. Some innovations can be carefully planned, scheduled and carried out. But in a crisis, change tends to take place much more quickly, especially when survival is at stake. While we would expect major changes to require careful consideration, it is surprising that it can be as difficult for small things to gain acceptance as for big ones.

Some people have quite strong opinions about the fabric of the church, such as the colour of the walls and paintwork, the type of carpet on the floor or the style of the chairs and communion vessels. It's only when you try to make changes that you find out just how important these things are to them.

Changes in tasks and relationships need very wise consideration. As people move away or take on new responsibilities, so others must replace them. A growing church may want an eldership as well as a diaconate. A pastor may need to be appointed to replace one who is leaving. Or a second person may be needed, perhaps a woman. In some churches the majority of members are quite unused to serving God because they've left it all to the leaders—they need to be encouraged to think about what gifts they themselves have been given.

Services have changed dramatically in some churches, but elsewhere there has been very little change so far. Things like a new hymn book, the use of Scripture Songs, or a different chair arrangement can present a major challenge to those trying to introduce them. There are other delicate issues too: tongues and prophecy; open times of praise; women participating audibly (what about 1 Tim 2?!); sacred dance; testimonies and interviews ('we prefer the solid exposition of the *word*!').

A church which is moving forward will be open to new projects. Some of those who had no bookstall are now thinking of having one (but should financial transactions take place on Sundays?!). When a congregation expands to a certain size it must consider the alternatives, such as splitting into two congregations, having two services or hiring a local school hall.

There will be as many views on what changes are good or bad as there are members of a church. We can have our own personal reasons why we favour this, or can't stand that. While we like to think of ourselves as logical

people, we really are not. Our inner feelings, temperament, prejudices and past experiences play a huge part
in influencing our attitudes and responses to proposed
changes. This is why it is so difficult for a congregation to
move forward together all at the same time!

10

Understanding Our Struggles

One of the biggest changes ever to be introduced into my own church has been the creating of structure within the communion service. For over fifty years, the hour-long service has been completely unplanned, with church members taking part as each was led by the Spirit. As the congregation grew to around 200, those who were more shy found it increasingly difficult to contribute publicly, and those who did so tended to be the same small number of people each week. The elders and deacons decided that twenty minutes of the service should be planned in advance, with a relatively large number of people being invited each week to join in, thus allowing much more of the congregation to be involved. As a consequence, the amount of time left completely open was cut down considerably.

The church was called together to hear an explanation of the new arrangements, and members were then invited to comment. The majority were happy with the new style of service and didn't feel the necessity to say very much, so those who spoke up first tended to be rather negative. I was intrigued that several people who held radically opposite viewpoints on almost every subject now seemed to be on the same side!

I thought about this afterwards and realized that the

reasons expressed for being cautious were quite diverse. For some long-standing church members, the change was a serious break with tradition and their sense of security was being threatened. Those who leaned more towards the charismatic side equally felt uneasy, but for a different reason—it would rob some of them of their freedom to take part.

As I tried to work out why others were unhappy with the change I could find no common factor. Each had his or her own unique reason for wanting to keep things as they were. The same was true of those who agreed with it.

Though they may not admit it, few people are truly objective about what they like and dislike. Those of us who have the responsibility of guiding a church will find the task more effective if we try to understand why people accept or reject new ideas. Then when we plan something new we will be able to bear in mind the reactions and feelings of those whose lives will be affected. Creating changes can be hazardous, but we can avoid disaster if we take the trouble to show sympathetic understanding towards those entrusted to our care.

Why do we resist change?

As we wrote earlier, each of us is a mysterious mixture of two persons. One eagerly seeks adventure but the other clings to what he knows. Some aspects of church life (like the use of a well-loved hymn book or the fact that the communion service is always in the morning) are very precious to us. If they are threatened in any way, then we may fight to preserve them. Sometimes new ideas fill us with inspiration and excitement. At other times, moving into the unknown causes great fear. We may wonder how the new arrangements will really work. Or we may worry that it will be just the thin end of the wedge—like the occasional use of a guitar for accompanying a Scripture Song. We may even think that a particular change might split the church.

Traditions are so strong and have developed over so many years that a church may no longer be functioning in line with Scripture. Slowly and without being aware of it, congregations can become ignorant of what the Bible really teaches about things like shared leadership, spiritual gifts and the role of women. Today many church leaders are re-examining the word of God and have concluded that there are some serious discrepancies between what they are doing and what the Bible teaches. Others genuinely think they are already basing their lives on Scripture and therefore resist change. They are blinkered to anything except their own long-held interpretation of it. For them, any change would be regarded as 'unscriptural' and must be fought at all costs.

We would all agree that the pharisees in New Testament times had closed minds. They were totally against anything which was contradictory to their opinions. Even twentieth-century Christians can be like that. Personal prejudice is hard to recognize in ourselves and even more difficult to break down.

I can remember the days in the mid seventies when one or two of us in our church began using the Revised Standard Version instead of the Authorized (King James) Version—there were some strong reactions from several people who regarded the KJV as the only reliable version. It was even worse when the Good News Bible was used publicly, not to mention the Living Bible! One or two people gave in because of the pressure and went back to reading only from the Authorized. Those of us who still felt we should use modern versions were requested by the elders to make it clear to the congregation just which version we were using. Thus peace reigned once again!

When people are genuinely contented with something as it is, they will be very reluctant to abandon it. Only when they feel some dissatisfaction with the present situation will they react favourably to an alternative, unless it is something really spectacular. It is extremely difficult to create change among people who are not to some degree unhappy about the way things are.

We all have emotional needs like belonging, purpose, love and significance. It's the way God made us. If any change seems likely to deprive us of one or more needs, then we will not find it easy to accept it—because deprivation causes emotional hurt. On the other hand, an idea which we believe fulfils an unmet need will be much more acceptable.

For example, why do some leaders, who possess a great deal of power, fight against having team leadership in their churches? Is it the fear that they will lose some of their significance? Why do people shrink from seeking church growth? Maybe they think they will be given less attention, because it will largely be directed towards new members. A simple decision to switch a lady's job of handing out biscuits to someone else can be a major catastrophe, because it robs her of a sense of purpose in the ladies' meeting.

Before trying to implement any change, we need to ask ourselves whether people's basic needs are going to be threatened in any significant way. If they are—light blue touch paper, stand back and take cover!

What will persuade people to accept new ideas?

You may feel that there are so many obstacles to change that you may as well give up. Keeping the system as it is will be far less trouble. So let's now look at the positive side.

It is a fact that most churches which have experienced radical changes have done so without major disasters! Generally, where the leaders have prayed and worked things out carefully, things have gone reasonably smoothly. While there are always negative factors which persuade people to play safe, there are also strong forces pulling us in a forward direction. It is those which we must harness.

As we have already observed, people resist changes which threaten an emotional need, but they welcome those which fulfil a felt need. Some who feel that they have no part to play in the local body of Christ may be pleased at the prospect of discovering their spiritual gifts because it will give them purpose and significance—so they will welcome this new emphasis in their church. Those who feel somewhat neglected in a fast-growing church may be very happy with the suggestion of meeting in members' homes, because they will receive considerably more pastoral care in a small group. There would also be more opportunity to show love to others, thus meeting that need to give love as well as receive it. Returning to our church meeting, I noticed that the proposed structured service was favoured by those who would love to be invited to make a two-minute contribution.

If what is being proposed seems really attractive, it will play a big part in persuading people that some aspect of the present is worth giving up, especially if the current situation is far from ideal. For example, my own church was becoming seriously overcrowded and this was causing frustration. The proposed extension to the chapel was estimated to cost £40,000—a great deal of money to some, which could have proved a serious stumbling block. But the dream of sitting in more space and comfort helped to remove the barriers to spending so much capital.

Some churches don't have a full-time minister because they feel happier without one. Yet they may agree to such an appointment if they believe that everyone will receive more effective pastoral care and that the quality of teaching will be better. Churches with only one group

of leaders (say elders) may eventually welcome the recognition of a second group to take care of some area of
church life when it becomes obvious that releasing the
elders from certain responsibilities will enable them to
function better.

No matter how good a suggestion may be, if it isn't
'sold' properly then it is less likely to receive a warm
welcome. No one wants to switch to something that
sounds boring! People like to be part of exciting new
ventures, and there is no reason why a change should not
be introduced with confidence and enthusiasm, because
that is infectious. Even so, people don't like things to be
'sprung' on them suddenly—they need time to let it
soak in, and the opportunity to discuss it.

What happens in a church when something new is announced?

When a change is first suggested there will be a wide
variety of initial responses, but as time goes on many
people will change their minds after reflecting on it.
Some will welcome it straight away, while others may
feel quite neutral. Moving towards the other end of the
scale, some people will say an immediate and loud
'No'! Others will go even further by actively trying to
prevent it from happening at all.

To those who are concerned to implement new ideas,
it may be of value to know roughly what to expect in a
congregation by way of response when a change is announced or suggested.

Although most people tend at first to regard any change
as bad news, there will always be a few who welcome
something new with wild enthusiasm. Some of them may
be newcomers who don't yet know enough about the
church to be able to weigh things up. Other enthusiasts
include what I would call 'shiftless' people who never

think anything through very deeply. Any novel idea will tend to appeal to them rather easily. One or two may be people who think you're absolutely the 'bee's knees' and that anything you say must be right. Oh for more of those—they make us leaders feel good! But beware!— all this can be quite misleading. A few strong 'Hear hears' or 'Amens' may sound like a majority opinion, but it probably isn't—so we mustn't pin all our hopes on such people.

At least 80% of church members will respond cautiously to change, and some may be hostile at first. They may even express their hostility on a rather personal basis towards the person who makes the suggestion or announcement. What people need is time to make up their minds. Some planned changes will need a longer time span than others. A New Year's Eve party may require only a month, but splitting the church into house groups could easily take a year.

People usually want to ask questions to find out how it will work and who will be affected. They like to weigh up the pros and cons of what they personally will gain or lose. On the whole, people rarely work things out objectively—it would be easier if they did, because we would know that their reactions and responses were concerned only with the good of the church rather than self-interest.

Some churches take votes, others simply get an overall impression of what the general feeling is like. If only about half the group is in favour of something, then it may not be wise to go ahead. A local baptist church held a referendum about appointing its first-ever pastor. The vote was roughly 50-50 and so the deacons decided not to go ahead at that particular time. In every church there will be a small number of people whose opinions are sought and valued by others. They might be officially-designated leaders, but they might not be. Because of their strong influence on other people, their support or otherwise is crucial as to whether an idea is accepted by the congregation or rejected by it. Even an 80% majority will be unworkable if those key individuals decided to hold out.

Just as there will be a minority who welcome an idea very rapidly, there will also be some at the other end of the spectrum. They may take ages to accept anything new, however trivial or harmless it may be. Almost any change threatens them. Eventually, most will decide to accept it, perhaps only grudgingly. Even so, one or two will not even go that far, but will actively try to hinder progress, or even leave the church over the issue.

For a church to move forward, its leaders have to be both bold and sensitive at the same time. Boldness carries both the risk of failure and the exciting prospect of success. (Success for a Christian congregation is when it is moving in the direction decided by God and communicated through the Spirit by various means.)

It is likely that we will move rather more slowly than some would like, but just a little too fast for others. If we are sensitive only to the feelings of the former we run the risk of a major upset. But if we drag our heels until every single person is in complete agreement, we shall make no progress at all. When people at one end of the spectrum feel somewhat uncomfortable because the church is not moving rapidly enough, and those at the opposite end feel that it is going too quickly, then we have probably got it right.

11

Moving Forward Together

Until about 1979, my church (Cranleigh Chapel) was a typical middle-of-the-road Open Brethren Assembly, with an almost static membership of around 100. According to good Brethren tradition we had no pastor, and an open-style communion service; women's voices were silent and discussion of the Holy Spirit was more or less taboo.

Over the next few years several areas of church life changed completely. We appointed a full-time pastor (called a pastoral co-ordinator). Soon, two elders presided over the communion service, and a couple of years later it was given a certain amount of structure. The ladies were invited first to take part in the mid-week prayer meetings, then at the breaking of bread service itself. Members to whom God may have revealed something were asked to share their prophecies with the elders who then passed on relevant matters to the church. As a result of conversions and some transfer growth we had to enlarge the chapel to accommodate a congregation of 200.

Despite the many changes in a comparatively short period of time there were surprisingly few serious problems and we only lost three church members. Although Cranleigh is referred to frequently in this chapter, it is only by way of illustration—it is not meant to be a blueprint for all to follow! While we humbly acknowledge that we have received a large measure of God's grace, it must be said that the changes which went well were also the result of prayerful and careful planning. I would like to share some of the details with you.

Where ideas come from

Where did the ideas come from which eventually led to changes taking place? I can recall mentioning some of them myself at elders' meetings. I actually instituted some very minor innovations without officially consulting anyone—like praying in modern English instead of Elizabethan. At the weekly prayer meeting I invited people to suggest their own topics for prayer rather than simply listing what I felt we should pray for.

Over the years suggestions have come from many sources; for example, from my fellow elders, the deacons, department heads and more often than not from members of the congregation not holding any particular leadership position. Some thoughts have emerged quite spontaneously as people have talked informally. Others have resulted from meetings involving leadership teams connected with youth work, junior church or women's work.

I have learnt to make haste slowly, even when I feel sure that an idea has come from God. Some things may take several years to come to fruition. Usually, it's wisest just to chat about an idea initially with just one or two people. Often they will bring it up for discussion later at a leaders' meeting and will then take the credit for it! There are other ways of dropping hints—like passing round some relevant literature. Or, if we are preachers, we can casually mention one or two ideas during a sermon to see if there is any response.

Perhaps we can learn a lesson from Nehemiah after he had learnt of the sad plight of the Jews in Jerusalem. He wept, mourned and fasted and said nothing to anyone at first. Eventually he got permission from the King to visit Jerusalem. He set out at night with a few close friends and inspected the broken walls of the city. No one else knew of the burden God had given him. Eventually he was so convinced that the task was God-given that he informed his fellow leaders, and finally the whole community began to rebuild the walls.

I realize that some readers may not be elders, deacons or PCC members and therefore have little opportunity to air their views where decisions are being made. May I suggest that you ask a leader to raise the matter on your behalf, or that you personally seek a hearing at the next leaders' meeting. At our own elders' meetings we frequently spend time with individual church members when they want to discuss an idea, a gripe or a career decision.

It is especially important not to be too pushy when you're new to a situation. It is usually wise to say and do nothing revolutionary for a few months or even a year or two. This is as true for pastors as it is for everyone else. I can remember making a nuisance of myself when I first arrived in a racially sensitive part of the USA. I had hardly had time to understand the complications of black-white relationships.

But when you think you're an expert at something it's easy to tell people what they should be doing. From 1964–70 I was involved in church planting in the UK and among North American whites and Indians. In 1979, I had attended a church growth conference, and since then I had read several books on the subject. To add to my imagined wealth of knowledge, I had recently finished co-editing a book on evangelism. Yes indeed, I knew what I was talking about! So when I was asked to advise on church planting during a recent visit to Nepal, I had all the answers:

'Invite an evangelist from another area, settle him

in a house, and ask him to go door-to-door.'

'You can't do that—houses and land rarely come up for sale as they do in the West—they are passed on from father to son. As for door-to-door work, he would probably be arrested if he did that!'

'All right then—why not use local Christians to do evangelism?'

'That won't work either, because the converts are all lepers or TB patients and as such are socially unacceptable. . . .'

And so it went on for the next two hours. At the end of the time I realized that I simply couldn't take ideas which had worked in the West and assume they were relevant to Nepal. One of the greatest weaknesses of those who have done something successfully, is the temptation to think, 'When we were at so-and-so we did it this way!'

Weighing up the suggestions

It is usually the responsibility of leadership groups to evaluate new ideas. There are four things which may happen to a suggested change.

1. Drop it for the time being, or even permanently.
2. Mention it briefly and informally among church members.
3. Hold a special meeting for detailed discussion among the congregation leading to a decision.
4. Agree to the idea and announce it to the church without prior consultation.

1. Sometimes a suggestion should be dropped completely, or its discussion postponed until a future occasion. Often there is insufficient time to talk about something new because it's getting late or other matters are more urgent. However, it is all too easy for such items to be forgotten by the next leaders' meeting. We are fortunate in having one elder who keeps track of everything and

includes postponed subjects on the next agenda, and another who keeps careful minutes and circulates copies.

Looking back over the records of the last few years, I can see that quite a number of our recent decisions relate to ideas which were floated several years ago. Sometimes one elder has to win over the others before we are ready as a group to move forward.

As you read this you may feel discouraged because some of your suggestions have not yet been adopted. May I suggest that if you are still convinced you can do no harm by quietly and persistently raising the issues. Above all, be patient!

2. It may be too soon for a long and serious discussion among church members even though the leaders are convinced that something is right. Under those circumstances it may be wise to mention the plan casually and briefly in order to give time for slow germination in people's minds. This could be done within a sermon, introduced as an item for prayer or mentioned informally at a church meeting whose main aim is to discuss something else. Some suggestions (especially if they concern delicate issues) may need to be aired several times until there is a groundswell of interest and approval.

3. When the time is right it is usual to call the church together for a longer discussion. Maybe a half day or whole day is appropriate or even a weekend at a conference centre. The method of arriving at a decision varies from one church to another. In the more democratic fellowships the church meeting makes decisions, often by means of a vote. In others the leaders listen carefully to all that is said and then go away prayerfully to make the decision.

This is how we appointed our very first 'pastor'. As elders we were rather reluctant to take a strong lead on such an important issue, even though we personally felt sure it was right. Somehow we wanted to see concrete evidence of strong support from the church. At the meeting the discussion went on for some time with almost total support. As we began to cover old ground again, one of the ladies spoke up: 'You are the elders. You have heard our comments. We trust you and so we'd like you to go from this meeting and do your job by making the decision.' And that's just what we did, and Elfed and Jackie are with us today!

4. Occasionally leaders may feel that a particular change needs to be set in motion without any prior consultation with the church. In this case, the purpose of the church meeting is simply to inform the people of the decision and to give the opportunity for asking questions.

On the whole, it is not a good thing to 'spring' major changes on people. Even if the leaders ultimately make the final decision, they still like to have time to weigh it up, to be consulted and to have their own ideas considered seriously, so that the final decision is more a joint one. People will be much more enthusiastic in supporting something when they have been involved in planning it, as opposed to a change presented to them as a *fait accompli*.

Sudden announcements don't always end up as disasters. Much depends on the atmosphere of the church meeting and more especially on the day-to-day relationships between the leaders and the led. It's all a matter of confidence and trust. Our elders' decision to invite women to participate audibly in the worship service was not publicly aired at all before it was announced. I was given the job of spelling it out. I prepared thoroughly beforehand, and took the time to explain it fully with adequate opportunity for comments. In addition every church member was given a duplicated set of notes summarizing what I had said. Similarly, when we invited those with prophecies to submit them to the elders (without prior consultation before we made the decision) there was little or no reaction. On the other hand when we told the church about structuring the communion service, some people did feel uncomfortable about the lack of any previous hint that this change was being considered.

Deciding what is appropriate

Whether a church makes decisions democratically or not makes little difference to the fact that God holds the leaders responsible for guiding the church towards discovering and following God's will. To do that, they need a combination of spiritual discernment and God-given reasoning.

Unfortunately, at most leaders' meetings very little time is spent in prayer. At best there is an opening prayer, before getting down to business. I'm not suggesting that it totally prevents God from revealing his will during the discussion, because it doesn't. But sometimes God may want to tell us there and then using supernatural means in addition to rational discussion. This process cannot be hurried. Listening to God is rarely an instantaneous exercise and often requires intense concentration. God may also want to show us things through other church members in the form of a prophecy, a word of knowledge or a verse of Scripture. Each of these potential revelations needs praying through as well as talking about.

Nor must we neglect the value of careful reasoning and thorough homework. We are not meant to rely solely on prophecies and the like. We need to make a list of possible alternatives and then decide which is the right one. Often this requires hard work in advance of the discussion. Some leadership groups set up small non-executive working groups (think tanks, sub-committees, steering committees) in order to spread the load of fact finding and listing possible courses of action. These groups don't normally make decisions but provide assistance to those who do. When we were deciding whether to set up cell groups in our church, five of us were asked to do a feasibility study and to present it to the next elders' meeting. Once again, Nehemiah has set a good example to follow. Before announcing anything he had worked out in advance some of the details of the rebuilding project and the resources needed.

To provide help in decision-making, more and more churches are inviting neutral outsiders to act as consultants. Recently several churches have asked me to visit them on this basis. There is one church in particular where I have a special relationship in which I have met with the leaders every year or two, on one occasion for a whole weekend. I have no executive authority over that church and its decisions, but I normally make a series of recommendations for them prayerfully to consider.

Sometimes heartless employers announce changes without being sensitive to the needs of their work force. We cannot behave like this because the congregation is God's family, not *our* employees. Their feelings, needs, fears and aspirations must be taken into account when we consider a new project. We must bear in mind how the proposal will affect them. If a church has undergone several changes in a short period of time, leaders must consider seriously whether they have the capacity to cope with yet another innovation in the near future.

Planning in advance of a church meeting

Let's assume that a group of leaders is reasonably convinced about the rightness of a particular change, and that they have already mentioned the idea informally some time ago. What is the next step? The obvious answer is to call a church meeting at the earliest possible date. It all sounds very straightforward, doesn't it.

In a real church composed of normal people it's not quite so simple as that. There will be several events which have to take place before the big discussion, and the setting of the date for a church meeting must allow enough time for them to occur. Some churches have a two-tier system of leadership (like elders and deacons, or the PCC and elders). The proposed change must be accepted by the second group before the church is asked to consider it seriously. Those individuals who exercise strong influence in the church need to be identified and arrangements made to talk to them privately in advance of the larger gathering. Others whom we anticipate will be strongly negative about the change would also appreciate a visit as a matter of courtesy. We probably won't win all of them over, but they will be pleased that we have considered their opinions worth listening to. Before discussing the participation of women in the communion service we visited several people for whom the change would be hard to accept. I can't say that each one changed his or her mind, but it did generate a large measure of genuine goodwill.

It is important to choose the right person to introduce the subject and the discussion which follows. However, we mustn't assume that it will be the same leader each time. What is important is to select the one who is the most appropriate for the occasion. Often a particular person will have the ability to put things across in a non-threatening manner, whereas another may wade in both feet first and cause difficulties.

It goes without saying (or does it?) that team loyalty among leaders is vital. Whatever disagreements there may have been in the privacy of the leaders' meeting, both in public and in personal conversation no leader should let it be known that he was the odd man out. The leadership must stand together, otherwise one or more disgruntled individuals will undermine the others, and cause people to question the credibility of the team.

At the meeting

The outcome of a public discussion will be strongly influ-
enced not only by who chairs it but also on the way it is led.
It will depend too on what happened in previous meetings
as well as the nature of the subject being talked about.
It's all a question of atmosphere and confidence. Are
people relaxed because the last few meetings were relaxed
and positive? Or have they recently experienced a disaster because someone steam-rollered them into a certain
decision? Maybe a bitter feud had developed. If so, we
need to take steps to reassure people that this time it will
be different, and to ensure that it actually happens.

On the whole, in churches where day-to-day relationships are warm, trusting and open, church meetings will
run smoothly. The higher the level of trust among the
congregation (and of the leaders), the bigger are the
changes which can be made. In an atmosphere of insecurity and suspicion, even a minor suggested change will
meet with resistance.

Back in the early seventies, I used to dread some of
our meetings. We only had them once a year. Some
people seemed to store up all their negative emotions
and criticisms during the rest of the year and then they
would burst out at the one and only opportunity we gave
them for open discussion. You will have heard of the
open season for grouse shooting. Well, church meetings
were open season for elder shooting. We were oversensi-
tive too in our handling of criticism because our defensiveness gave the impression that we were unwilling to
listen to people's criticisms. Now we have several meetings
a year, whenever there is something we need to talk
through. We also have more social occasions which help
to cement relationships.

By the late seventies things had changed for the better.
As people opened up their lives to each other, and the

elders became more secure, we began to look forward to our get-togethers. Gradually, people began to trust us as we sought to guide them towards the right decisions. They also knew that we genuinely valued their own contributions and carefully considered them when we next met.

The attitude and expectation of the person leading the discussion is all-important, because people will detect whether he is optimistic or pessimistic. We do need to be realistic about the fact that people usually resist change at first, so we must handle this natural resistance without getting upset. But there is a world of difference between being prepared for this normal reaction and expecting outright and possibly hostile rejection — because our expectation will influence the way we outline the project. If we present something assuming from the start that it will fail, then it probably will! I don't mean that we must use a slick sales technique. Far from it! We just need to talk about it with enthusiasm, and have a willingness to answer people's questions and criticisms.

I vividly remember a disastrous approach to the Bible College by a representative of a youth movement that was looking for full-time staff. Unfortunately he spent the whole time defending the organization against possible attack from those of us who were listening. He shouldn't have done so because it gave us the impression that the movement was no good. The result? No one volunteered to join!

Clear communication is vital if we are to have a relaxed and constructive discussion afterwards. We should make plain the purpose of the meeting from the start. If an idea is merely to be floated with no decision being reached for some time, then we should say so. Or maybe the leaders have been discussing something in detail for quite a while and are sharing their thoughts with a view to a decision being made at the church meeting (or later when they meet as a group). Another possibility is that the leaders want to announce something which they have already decided, and the purpose of the meeting is for questions and clarification only. (Normally this would be the last stage of a series of discussions, starting with a low key informal presentation.)

When we decided to create structure within the communion service, the chairman of the meeting talked concisely and logically about how it would work. What he didn't do was to start off by saying that the elders had already made the decision. This was unfortunate because it was only after some time that one of the church members raised the question. The answer made him feel rather negative and he was not inclined to ask any more questions.

Once the aim of the meeting is clear people can relax because they feel secure. We must also choose our words and tone of voice carefully. For example, it is better to talk about 'our' and 'we' rather than 'mine' and 'I'. When a decision is announced as a *fait accompli* we should avoid a 'thus saith the Lord' approach. There is a big difference between presenting something enthusiastically and ramming it down people's throats in an authoritarian manner. Even enthusiasm has to be tempered by humility and tact.

In a genuinely open discussion there will be some disagreement, because you can't please all of the people all of the time. (In fact you should be suspicious if there isn't any, because it probably means that people feel stifled and are afraid to speak up.) Complaints are not necessarily a sign that a church is falling apart. We should welcome them because they show that people feel free to voice dissent. We must never think of church members as puppets on strings being pulled by the leaders. When they express reservations it is in the hope that we will consider their viewpoints as important and therefore will affect the final outcome.

Nor must a leader regard disagreement as necessarily a personal attack on him. Oversensitivity in private or public leads either to defensiveness or retaliation. When leaders have become mature enough to handle healthy differences of viewpoints among themselves, they will find it easier to cope with disagreements from church members.

Some people get very worried about publicly aired disagreements (even cordial ones) because they assume that they inevitably lead to division. This is especially true when an opposite viewpoint is expressed strongly. One of the tasks of leadership is to help people to be strong enough to allow others the right to think differently. We need to teach people the meaning of passages like Romans 14, where Paul says that where matters not concerning fundamental doctrines are concerned, we must permit people to hold their own viewpoints without condemning them.

There are various ways of handling a discussion. It doesn't have to be done in a large group. Sometimes, after an issue has been explained, the congregation could split up into groups, each led by an elder. It's often easier to talk among ten than a hundred.

Sometimes we will be able to help people to examine their own negative reactions constructively. But watch out for black eyes! People don't always like it. Most of us feel perfectly justified in the way we present our thoughts. We usually prefer not to admit that we felt threatened or that we were about to be denied one of our basic human needs. Yet as a community becomes more trusting, honest discussion of feelings can be very profitable.

After the meeting

During the course of the discussion (or even afterwards)

it may be necessary to consider revising the original plan or even dropping it for the time being. The latter may seem like a defeat, but there is no need for leaders to feel ashamed. It is better to abandon something or postpone it rather than stubbornly pushing ahead when either the change itself or the timing is inappropriate.

Those who generate new ideas don't like what they consider to be compromise, because they tend to think that their plans (including all the details) have been infallibly received from God. This can cause them to be inflexible. Often their reluctance to adapt their plans stems not from divine authority but from pride or a sense of threat. Such an attitude is counter-productive because it makes people resentful and sometimes hostile.

Even minor concessions can make some changes more acceptable. I know of a church which occasionally introduced some very mild sacred dance into its services. It wasn't announced in advance so people didn't know beforehand. This didn't matter for those who enjoyed dance, but it was a different story for those who were against it. Rather than abandon dance altogether, it was decided to announce such events a week in advance so that those who strongly objected to it would have the opportunity to stay away on the occasions when it took place.

Another way out of a dilemma is to regard something new as an 'experiment' lasting, say, six months. It's much less threatening than something which looks permanent because people know that if it is a flop it can be abandoned without loss of face. Most 'experiments' do in fact continue after the trial period. That six months is especially helpful to those people who initially don't want to commit themselves to a permanent change. It gives them time to adjust.

Defusing may be as necessary after a decision has been reached as it was beforehand. There will always be one or two who remain unhappy about the way things are going and would like time to share their views with a couple of leaders.

If a change is right, most people will ultimately accept it. Some people may hold out for a very long time. Be patient! We must give them every opportunity to change their minds without loss of face. Even when they have come round, it's best to avoid reference at a later date to the fact that they once opposed something.

But what about casualties? No, I'm not referring to black eyes! By that I mean the small minority who leave the church as the result of change. The latest innovation may not be the most dramatic but is the straw that breaks the camel's back. Some may cluster together as a disenchanted group, possibly storming out in a cloud of dust. Others will huff and puff their way out individually. Some quietly creep away never to be seen again.

It is possible to be so scared of losing even a single member that a church will opt for a cheap peace. The result is stagnation, because the majority of important changes involve a price of some kind, though it will not always be the loss of one or two members. If outward harmony is our main goal, we can easily fall into the trap of allowing a dominant minority to rule the rest of the church, who remain silent and submissive for the sake of peace. True, peace has been preserved, but at the expense of growth and progress.

In a church where there is trust and maturity there should be few casualties and a minimum of deep hurt. But supposing someone honestly feels that he really cannot cope with things as they are or are going to be? It may be quite reasonable to discuss an orderly transfer to a less progressive church, where he or she will feel more at home. We once made such an arrangement with the leadership of a nearby church after an older couple graciously explained their predicament to us. It was a painful break after many years in the same church but it turned out to be for the best.

We mustn't assume that once a change has been instituted nothing further needs to be done. Most new schemes have teething troubles and we need to be ready to make alterations to the original plan. In my own church we began with ten cell groups among 150 people. A year later we had to reduce them to nine, because one was sparsely attended. We also made changes in the composition of some groups to provide more balance and to incorporate new church members.

It's great to get a project accepted and actually operating. It's part of the process of growth and renewal. Yet we must avoid the temptation to see it as something that remains for ever. Otherwise when another change is needed, we will cling so fiercely to this one, that further progress is blocked. In some ways we must regard church life as being a cycle, as it is with nature: birth, growth, decay, death . . . birth, growth, decay, death. . . . We can never attain the ultimate pattern of church life which will last for ever. If we feel we have done so, then we have failed, because we will one day be unwilling to permit the death of something which is new and exciting now, so that another venture may develop. What we must do is follow God's will for today, and listen to what he wants to say to us about tomorrow.

Ears to Hear
Listening to God and others

by Derek Copley and Mary Austin

Most of us are very good at talking—we've had a lifetime's experience. Day after day we expect others to listen to what we have to say.

But how good are we at *listening?*

This book was born out of the conviction that if we learn how to listen for God's voice, and obey it when we hear it, then we will find a new effectiveness in listening to others. As we learn to show real love and acceptance to others so we will become more like the greatest listener of all, Jesus Christ.

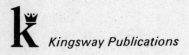

Kingsway Publications

A Man Under Authority
Qualities of Christian Leadership

by Charles Sibthorpe

If you believe that God has called you to a position of leadership—or may be calling you now—this book is for you.

Charles Sibthorpe shows that true leadership is by example: as God works *in* us, so he is enabled to work *through* us. All who are called to leadership within the church—elders and deacons, clergy and ministers, house-group leaders, youth workers, leaders of praise and worship—are invited here to experience a deeper encounter with the living God and so enjoy a ministry that is right at the heart of God's loving purposes.

Charles Sibthorpe has seen the power of God transform both his own ministry and that of many others. He is now an elder at the Bethany Fellowship in Sussex and is responsible for leadership training at The Hyde Leaders' Weeks.

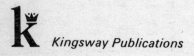

Kingsway Publications